Capturing Heaven:

Why You Don't Have to Suffer

Matt Donnelly

WORD & SPIRIT
PUBLISHING

Capturing Heaven: Why You Don't Have to Suffer

ISBN: 978-1-685730-07-9

Published by Word and Spirit Publishing
P.O. Box 701403
Tulsa, Oklahoma 74170
wordandspiritpublishing.com

Printed in the United States of America.

Contents

Acknowledgment

A project of any size or success is never a solitary effort or the proverbial "one man show." It is a collaboration of many parts and influences coming together to form something new. I am greatly honored to have written this book, but so many other people have contributed to its content, creativity, and publication. First, I would like to thank my wife, Tammy, for always pushing me, encouraging me, and making me better. God's blessing is most manifested in my life through her. She has been so patient, putting in tireless hours of discussion, reading, and listening to me retell the same point in a particular chapter until I was satisfied with the outcome. Without her, this book would never have happened! Greatest wife in history!

I also want to thank so many mentors, coaches, and ministers of the Gospel who have come before me, some who I have known personally and others only through a book or a sermon. Those who previously blazed trails in Truth have been instrumental in my life, to the development of a firm foundation of sound doctrine centered on Jesus and a catalyst for the things discussed in this book.

I also want to recognize Molly and Dave Hill, who supported this project before it even got off the ground. They have contributed in so many ways, and I am honored for their help. Thank you for your faith, love, and encouragement! Also, I want to recognize Dan and Elaine Brewer, who have been a great source of support and inspiration. Their infectious passion for the Gospel and the Kingdom has been a fountainhead of inspiration for us. Thank you for your friendship and all the ways you have supported Tammy and me!

Finally, I want to thank God for so many friends and family who have supported this undertaking in everything from words of encouragement to taking some time to read a portion of the rough draft and offer constructive feedback. All was appreciated and integral to the finished product.

Like a good recipe, every part—every ingredient—is essential to what is ultimately served in the meal. Thank You, Jesus, for surrounding Tammy and me with so many loving people. God has truly blessed us beyond our imagination! God bless you!

Introduction

"Cerebral palsy," the doctor declared in that professional way that lends no emotion in its tone.

The tone that comes from so many years of delivering the life-devastating diagnosis. My mom and dad had just received heartbreaking confirmation from the acting physician concerning my brother's condition.

Mike was the third of three children. My sister and I were both under three years old when my parents found out they were pregnant again with him. Mike was born on February 7, 1982, in Raleigh, North Carolina. There were some complications in the delivery, but everything appeared to be normal at that time. But fast-forward twelve months, and on that awful day, the news was confirmed that Mike had neurological damage that affected his movements. The disability with which he was diagnosed is called cerebral palsy, or CP for short.

My parents were Christians who had been miraculously saved out of the party scene of the 1970s when they found

Jesus. They had both grown up in Catholic homes; my dad came from a large midwestern Kansas family with seven brothers and sisters, while my mom came from the East Coast, having been raised in Raleigh, North Carolina. She had both a younger and an older brother; she and her siblings had all been adopted at a very young age.

My mom and dad were set free from drugs and a sinful lifestyle and were filled with the Holy Spirit. They saw an instant change and began to live their lives completely for Christ. All of this began from reading a Christian tract they found on the street that had been dropped by a passerby. They were young in the Lord and in life, only being in their twenties when Mike was born. My mom used to say, "I had three children in diapers, all at the same time." It was the best of times, and it was the worst of times, depending on the day and the time. God had revealed Himself to my parents in such a real way, and yet there was a lurking enemy that would tear their lives apart.

One can only imagine the hurt, guilt, and confusion that strikes with that kind of medical report. People can ask many questions when faced with devastating news:

"Where are You, Lord?"

"What did I do wrong?"

"Why would You allow this to happen to our son?"

These questions and many more come rushing through the mind like a flurry of hornets, attacking without mercy.

A well-meaning Christian may unequivocally say, "God is in control." But that statement may stir an equal share of comfort and confusion depending on the circumstances one may be facing. On the one hand, a man just lost his job and does not know how he is going to feed his family. He comes home to tell his wife of the newfound challenge before them, and she reaches across the kitchen table to take his cold, nervous hand in her own. She soothingly states, "Don't worry. God is in control." With a vulnerable optimism emerging through his malaise, he musters a smile and squeezes her hand a little tighter, as if he is trying to harvest a small portion of his wife's positive attitude and plant it within his own discouraged heart.

We can see there is a type of comfort in the truth that God is bigger than anything we face and that He is personally attending to our lives with His fatherly care. We should set our faith on our heavenly Father. He is all-good, and He is all-powerful. We have been created to depend on Him, to run to Him with every need or desire, knowing that He is the answer. Like children, we never outgrow His provision. God's Kingdom is based on this faith. God is sovereign in our faith in Him to handle the problems of life. As we turn to Him with this kind of faith, His power truly influences the outcomes—and the outcomes are in our favor 100 percent of the time. God is in control when we turn to Him and nothing else.

I remember a time when I was trying to handle things in my own energy and wisdom. Needless to say, I messed it all up. The problems only got worse, and I found myself in a deeper hole than when I had started. Then I finally turned my attention on God and away from the pain. I praised Him as God and exalted Him in song. I was depressed and lost, but bits and flashes of illumined rays streamed into my soul as I praised the Lord. His light pulled me from a suffocating depression into gleaming freedom. As I praised Him, answered prayer was the result. Praise exalted God in my personal life. God has a throne in heaven, but is He enthroned in your heart?

On the other hand, consider the following scenario: A child loses her loving Christian parents in a terrible car wreck, and she has to live with relatives who end up abusing her. She becomes a drug-addicted atheist, hating God for "taking away" her parents and leaving her in her own personal hell. She dies without healing or hope, overdosing in a dirty motel bathroom, and the Church's response is "God is in control"?

Is He?

In what way is God in control?

Is there another power at work? Does God permit evil or cause it? Does He will tragedy to take place? If God is behind everything, then where is the devil in all this mess? Or are God and the devil working together, as some preachers and theologians claim?

In the Body of Christ, there is much confusion about trials and tribulations and how God uses them in our lives. When referencing trials and tribulations as coming from God, one of the most cited texts in the entire Bible is the book of Job. The book of Job has been misunderstood and often misquoted for hundreds of years. These misunderstandings have come from the desire that is in all people to understand why bad things have happened to them or to those whom they love. There seems to be a comfort in believing that "the bad thing that is happening to me (no matter how painful or tragic) serves a good purpose and fits into the overall plan that God has destined for my life." In fact, most people would rather believe that a bad thing happening to them is for a good purpose than even to understand how to reverse the problem. (Through Jesus, you can stand in authority and change the situation to reflect something truly good.) This belief, that trials and tribulations are God's teachers in our life, is rooted in man's philosophy multiplied by external experiences. It is not supported by a firm foundation of Scripture. People, specifically Christians, have experiences in their lives that end in tragedy, pain, or death, and they look to the Bible to explain why this bad thing was really good from an eternal perspective. They will ask the question, "Why do bad things happen to good people?" Then, to answer that question, they will search the Bible and inevitably begin to draw conclusions—*false* conclusions—from different Scriptures that are misunderstood or lifted out of their context. Once again, the most-used text in this exercise is the book of Job. Why is the book of Job used in this way? Because, on the surface, without digging too deep into the details of the story, the book of Job appears to confirm an experience similar to that of countless suffering people: Job, a godly man who experiences terrible tragedy and loss, spends a great deal of time looking for the answer to the question, "Why is this happening to me?"

Job reels in his pain and suffering, desperately looking for what divine law he has violated to bring such tragedy into his life. You can sum up his search with one question: "Why are bad things happening to a good person?" People often ask that very question or something similar. This mystery has plagued mankind for ages: Why do the righteous suffer? Christians have looked to Job to answer that question, and they find a kind of comfort by relating to Job. The prevailing view is that God, in His eternal wisdom, has planned something amazing for our lives, but suffering through evil is necessary to achieve this ultimate goal. This kind of thinking sounds as if it's deep, or shrouded in some sort of religious, esoteric wisdom. It does not provide a conclusive answer; it only warms the suffering saint with the idea that there is purpose to their suffering. Unfortunately, this leaves the person shackled to their problem with no hope of relief. They stay on the religious "hamster wheel" believing that "the suffering" they are enduring is the plan of God. And for as long as that understanding is maintained, the person can never access freedom.

The book of Job has been misapplied for far too long. This is a book rich with redemptive truth because it is based on Jesus and the Good News found in the New Testament. Unlocking God's message in this book will free people to take authority over their circumstances and to be set free from the attack of the enemy. In the following chapters, we will look at what God has truly said in the book of Job and rightly divide the word of truth.

Chapter 1

Job's Top Ten

Many misunderstandings surrounding Job's experience are rooted in context, or rather, in the lack thereof. The events and circumstances featured in the book of Job are so very different from what we experience today. Some Christians have read the book of Job with a sincere heart, looking for answers with a desperation that grows those very answers they seek out of little to no scriptural context. Like we witness in modern American media, a breaking news story reported with little investigation all too often lends itself to misconceptions and false conclusions. We live in a world that can look one way until there is a closer examination of all the information. Most of us have heard of some tragic story of a man or woman locked up in prison for twenty-plus years who was eventually set free after being falsely accused and then wrongly convicted on circumstantial evidence. Why were they in jail in the first place? Usually, the acting investigator approached the case with an agenda, a preconceived idea, or good old-fashioned tunnel vision. The facts were painting the picture that the detective already had in his or her mind. What eventually set the innocent man or woman free? Someone approached the evidence with a fresh perspective. They opened the case file and began to see if there was anything missed or overlooked at the time of the investigation. The information was there all along, but it remained undiscovered because there was an objective already in motion that would not allow further exploration. Many times, when there has been a serious crime committed, there is so much emotion that drives the community and the police that it can lead to a false conviction.

It is a similar situation when tragedy or sickness strikes a family or an individual. We often look for clues that comfort. We have all been guilty of finding answers in the Bible that we wanted to find, whether they were there to be found or not. We see things in the Scripture that line up with a picture already painted in our minds from pain and suffering. Because of this, many have unknowingly put God on trial and falsely convicted Him for things He was not responsible for. Just as a weary traveler might gaze upon a thirst-inspired desert mirage, we see what we want or need to see and not what is actually there. We drink deeply of the sand-filled delusion, believing we have satiated our thirst, only to discover we are worse off than before. My objective in this chapter is to list the top-ten things that will shed some light on the time in which Job lived and some of the "whys" to the "whats" in Job. This list is not exhaustive, but in my opinion, it is relevant information if we are to pull truth from the pages of this sacred story.

1. *Job lived about the same time as Abraham.*

Because the book of Job seems to appear suddenly in the middle of the Old Testament, many Christians may assume that Job was written much later than it was. Job is considered, by many scholars, to have lived around the time of Abraham, Isaac, or Jacob (approximately 2100 to 1900 B.C.). One proof is that Job was performing his own sacrifices (very similar to the worship of the Patriarchs) instead of sacrificing at the Tabernacle or the Temple, which God would mandate as the only acceptable mode of offering under the Mosaic covenant through the Levitical priesthood. Also, Job is believed to have lived over two hundred years before he eventually died. He lived another 140 years after his adult children were killed. A two-hundred-year lifespan is, again, in line with what Scripture records about Abraham and the Patriarchs.

2. *Job's trial lasted a short time.*

When people look to Job as an example of righteous suffering, frequently most of Job's life is ignored or drowned out by the overwhelming intensity of his trials. Job lived over two hundred years, and most of that time was spent living in prosperity, protection, and health—blessings from God! When studying the trials of Job, the common consensus is that his hardships lasted about six months. In fact, if Job lived two hundred years or more and his sufferings lasted only six months, then Job lived 99.75 percent of his life tremendously blessed by the Lord! Someone suffering twenty to thirty years, or most of their lifetime, has very little in common with Job and his experiences.

3. *Job had no mediator.*

Job lived before Christ—and even before Moses. He lived during a time when humanity was without a priesthood.

> *Neither is there any daysman betwixt us,*
> *That might lay his hand upon us both.*
>
> —Job 9:33 KJV

A "daysman" was an arbitrator between two parties, whose job it was to help judge who was right and who was wrong.

> *If only there were someone to mediate between us,*
> *someone to bring us together.*
>
> —Job 9:33 NIV

Job's cry was the petition of the collective heart of humanity: If only there was Someone who could stand between us and God! Spoiler alert: Jesus has become our Great High Priest before God! He is the Advocate between us and the Father.

4. *Job not only regained his health, his wealth, and his family, but it was all doubled after his time of suffering.*

According to Job 42:10–17, Job was not a miserable little Christian, stumbling through life, entirely defined by his tragedy. His is a story of a man of triumph. If he lived today, Job would be on all the talk shows and lecture tours, telling the story of how he rose from the literal ashes to unimaginable financial and social success. He would be invited to mega-churches to describe the "what, when, where, and how" of his prosperity. Job's tale is a success story, but many only think of him in terms of his loss.

5. *Job was a "servant" of God (Job 1:8), but he did not have a true relationship with God.*

According to scholars, the name *Job* means "without a Father." The entire book was written to show man's plight without God as his Father. If Jesus came to show us the Father, the book of Job was written to demonstrate that even for a man who did everything right, it was still not enough. He believed in God and served God—but that's where it stopped. We, living in the New Testament Church, are called the "children of God" if we have received Jesus and He has made us new creatures. Job missed this all-important experience. Job represents Fatherless humanity and their plight in the time before Christ.

6. *The apostles did not view Job's tragedies as a blueprint for God's will concerning sickness and loss.*

When the apostle James refers to Job in James 5:10–12, he refers to two main lessons from Job's life: Job's patience, and "the end of the Lord." "The Lord is very pitiful and full of tender mercy."

Nowhere does James look to Job's sufferings as a blueprint of Christian expectation, other than to use him as an example of patience during persecution. James, a few verses later, is found writing some of the clearest verses on guaranteed healing from God through the prayer of faith. Job's sickness had no influence on James's theology on healing. Job's sickness and tragedy was a captivity from Satan, not a blessing from God!

> *Brothers, take the prophets who spoke in the Lord's name as an example of suffering and patience. See, we count as blessed those who have endured. You have heard of Job's endurance and have seen the*

> *outcome from the Lord. The Lord is very compassionate and merciful.*
>
> —James 5:10–11 HCSB

James relates Job's experience as something more related to persecution than to God's will for our bodies and our health. James uses the word *suffering* to describe the persecution of the prophets, and Job is included in that passage as an example of the righteous suffering unjustly. Several verses later, James wrote about the Christian response to suffering and sickness:

> *Is anyone among you suffering? He should pray. Is anyone cheerful? He should sing praises. Is anyone among you sick? He should call for the elders of the church, and they should pray over him after anointing him with olive oil in the name of the Lord. The prayer of faith will save the sick person, and the Lord will restore him to health; if he has committed sins, he will be forgiven.*
>
> —James 5:13–15 HCSB

Once again, James uses the same word used to describe suffering earlier in the chapter when referring to persecution. He instructs those who are suffering to pray. Contrast his response to the sick: He does not include them in the "suffering" category. He instructs them to call for the elders, who will pray the prayer of faith, and through this, the sick Christian is promised healing and forgiveness. James does not look to Job as an example of effective prayer or as a pattern demonstrating God's will for Christians concerning healing.

7. *Job lived before there was any written Scripture.*

Job had no Bible. He was only a follower of God because others had told him about God. God had not revealed Himself to Job, so Job did not truly know God in a personal way.

> *I have heard of thee by the hearing of the ear.*
>
> —Job 42:5 KJV

Job did not even have the book of Job to which to refer! He did not know any of the heavenly discourse that took place between God and Satan prior to his captivity. He had no true revelation of God from His Word. He had no promises to stand upon in faith or Scriptures to turn for comfort.

8. *Job's trials were called a "captivity."*

These tragedies are never characterized as forms of divine blessing, but rather a satanic assault on Job and his family. Some in the Church have glorified Job's travails as God's plan for his life.

> *And the LORD turned the captivity of Job….*
>
> —Job 42:10 KJV

This plan of God never included pain or suffering. God's plan was for mankind to live in a garden, with no death or demise—two perfect people to fellowship together with Him for all eternity. What brought pain into the world? It was not God who willed it, but Adam. Adam and Satan made a pact around the knowledge of good and evil. The Lord is good, period.

9. *Job was freed from his captivity.*

Job's captivity ended when he caught a revelation of God and prayed for his friends, who had falsely accused him of unrighteousness, assuming the destruction of his life was evidence to support their untrue claims.

> *I have heard of thee by the hearing of the ear:*
> *But now mine eye seeth thee.*
>
> —Job 42:5 KJV

> *And the LORD turned the captivity of Job, when he prayed for his friends: also the LORD gave Job twice as much as he had before.*
>
> —Job 42:10 KJV

The pain and the suffering had no purpose or meaning. It taught Job nothing. The difference occurred when God showed up and revealed Himself. Job was not a more spiritual person for having experienced loss and disease that ultimately led to his agony. Instead, he became spiritual when he encountered God. He suddenly possessed power in his prayer life when he acted on the command of God and not on his own fears! Job saw the victory when he took his eyes off himself and fixed them on the living God. Job was delivered when he took his attention off his problems and began to pray for others.

10. *Job is never referenced in Scripture for his faith.*

Hebrews 11 chronologically takes us through a history of faith, from Abel to Rahab, but oddly, Job is left out of the list. Job is mentioned in James 5, not for his faith, but for his patience. Elijah is mentioned in the same chapter as an example of the "prayer of faith." Job is related to suffering persecution with patience, but Elijah is brought up as an example of effective faith and prayer with a special reference toward divine healing!

Job's own testimony reveals he acted in fear rather than faith.

> *For the thing I greatly feared has come upon me,*
> *And what I dreaded has happened to me.*
>
> —Job 3:25 NKJV

The Septuagint describes the depth of Job's fear:

For the terror of which I meditated has come upon me, and that which I had feared has befallen me.

—Job 3:25 Brenton LXX

This fear had become Job's meditation. Faith was not a part of anything Job practiced. Instead, he was faithful to offer sacrifices for his children every day after each of their family dinners. These dinners were probably in celebration of the birthdays of the different family members. But Job worried about a misstep with God concerning his children's actions during the festivities, so he offered burnt offerings on an altar out of great fear for their spiritual and physical well-being. What drove him to pull animals from his herd and offer them to God? It was not the Holy Spirit leading him, nor was it an act of faith. He had "meditated" on—he was imagining—the idea of his children cursing God, and some fiery judgment pouring out of heaven to destroy them for their sin. He lay there at night upon his bed, unable to sleep, ruminating over this potential reality. He thought on this thing until it consumed him with a terror that finally drove him to action. His fear was a kind of faith in reverse. He believed in the reality of such terrible possibilities that he acted in such a way as if they were true; that is faith…but not faith in God!

Chapter 2

How Do You Build a House?

Job is a unique book in the Bible because it gives us one of the clearest pictures of the activity of heaven in the Old Testament. We are given the perspective of a courtroom reporter sitting on the sidelines listening in to a dialogue between God and Satan. This conversation between the Lord and the devil has been misused and even abused to build a false narrative about God's dealings with mankind. Like Job, men and women have frequently put God on trial in an attempt to justify themselves or to find meaning in their pain. They have maligned God's character and minimized Him. How has this ancient book been used to misinform so many? Ministers and mature Christians alike have read these Scriptures with veils over their eyes. They have interpreted these verses in darkness. Everything must line up with Jesus and who He is as revealed by the Gospel. Moses must line up with Jesus. Isaiah must line up with Jesus. Job must line up with Jesus, as well! False doctrines are birthed when we isolate Scripture from the revelation of Jesus Christ! There is no way to walk in truth without the Truth. Jesus is the Light of the World! That means we cannot truly see anything without Him shining upon our hearts. Too many theologians and preachers separate their understanding of different books of the Bible from their understanding and knowledge of Jesus. Jesus is called the Chief Cornerstone:

> *And are built upon the foundation of the apostles and prophets, Jesus Christ himself being the chief corner stone.*
>
> —Ephesians 2:20 KJV

> *Wherefore also it is contained in the scripture, Behold, I lay in Sion a chief corner stone, elect, precious: and he that believeth on him shall not be confounded.*
>
> —1 Peter 2:6 KJV

> *This is the stone which was set at nought of you builders, which is become the head of the corner.*
>
> —Acts 4:11 KJV

Jesus is the Chief Cornerstone. That means He is what every other stone must line up with to be accurate and correct. The apostles and the prophets are part of the foundation. Every verse in the Bible was written by either an apostle or a prophet. Every verse is from God and is truth. All of this is true, but there is a caveat: Every verse only reveals its truth in the light of Christ! If a person makes Job or Moses or even Paul the Chief Cornerstone, then the building is not going to be square. It is going to be out of alignment! We must start with Jesus and then interpret each prophet or apostle's writings as the Word of God, as it lines up with Jesus!

> *But the word of the Lord endureth for ever. And this is the word which by the gospel is preached unto you.*
>
> —1 Peter 1:25 KJV

The Word of God can only be preached by the Gospel. The Gospel is the Good News about who Jesus is and what He has done for you and me. The Gospel is good and powerful because it transforms a human being into a son of God when he hears and believes upon this Good News! The Gospel brings the truth of every Scripture to light, and we see God for the first time truly revealed to mankind. You cannot know God until your eyes are fixed on Jesus and the Gospel revelation.

Men have accused God of making Job sick or allowing Job to be sick for His purposes. The Gospel unveils the reality of this claim, and it is wrong on every level. Jesus went everywhere healing and forgiving. Jesus did this as the physical representation of the Father's nature. Jesus did not test people's faith by leaving them in their disease. He did not pass by those who were suffering while proclaiming a mysterious divine plan was being executed. No! He simply healed and healed and kept on healing all who put their faith in Him! Jesus prospered Peter's business. He certainly did not dry up all the fish in the sea to make Peter into a better disciple. He saved His disciples from storms, fed them, provided abundantly for them and their families, paid their taxes, healed their in-laws, and empowered them to have victory over devils and infirmity! He challenged them to believe and not fear! Jesus revealed the Father and His Kingdom. Prophets and Old Testament saints together longed to live in that time that the disciples then and the Church now experiences. God did not purpose or allow some attack of the devil to destroy Job's life so He could teach him some kind of moral lesson. There was no predestined purpose in the pain. There is an amazing revelation in the book of Job that will transform and even empower you to stand against the devil, victorious, when you line up its truths with what Jesus now has revealed. You cannot properly see Job's truths until you turn to Jesus and behold Him first. Job is a piece of the puzzle that fits nicely in the place where it was designed to fit. You will never understand the "puzzle" of the Scriptures in Job—or any other Scriptures—until you have your "end pieces" in place. Christ is the Border of the picture puzzle God has drawn for humanity! If those border pieces are not in place, we will attempt to make pieces of the puzzle fit where they do not belong. Or we will isolate one piece of the puzzle from the rest of the picture and determine the whole image from something partial and incomplete. Listen to Paul's own indictment against Israel when they read and interpreted Scripture without the light of Christ:

> *But their minds were blinded: for until this day remaineth the same vail untaken away in the* ***reading of the old testament****; which vail is done away in Christ. But even unto this day, when* ***Moses is read****, the vail is upon their heart. Nevertheless when it shall turn to the Lord, the vail shall be taken away.*
>
> —2 Corinthians 3:14–16 KJV, emphasis mine

Paul states that when they were reading the Old Testament Scriptures, there was a covering that blinded them from seeing the truth. When they turned to Jesus, the covering was removed, and the glory of the Light revealed the truth in every Scripture! When the Bible is studied without Christ, it is a darkened book that will be confused by its interpreters and confusing to its audience. Some of the most cursed teachings and beliefs have been extracted from its pages by unilluminated men. Someone may say that Paul is referring to salvation in these verses, and I would agree that is the initial "turning to the Lord" that is needed. In *everything* there must be a turning to the Lord. Christians who are saved and going to heaven still must make a conscious decision to turn to Jesus in everything, including the rest of the Scriptures.

> *Trust in the LORD with all thine heart;*
> *And lean not unto thine own understanding.*
> *In all thy ways acknowledge him,*
> *And he shall direct thy paths.*
>
> —Proverbs 3:5–6 KJV

Light does not show up on the path from God until we trust in God and not our own understanding. We must acknowledge Him in *all our ways*. That's when Light explodes onto the scene. That's when a trustworthy understanding of God's Word is discovered.

Again, I want to quote 1 Peter 2:6 (KJV):

> *Wherefore also it is contained in the scripture, Behold, I lay in Sion a chief corner stone, elect, precious: and he that believeth on him shall not be confounded.*

There is no confusion, shame, or disillusionment when someone puts their faith in Christ alone as the Chief Cornerstone of the building. Faith, even in Scripture, if not lined up with Jesus and who He is, can bring confusion into your relationship with God and the Bible. The gospel of Luke narrates a situation in which the disciples misapplied Scripture to their own situation because they did not line up with Jesus first.

> *And sent messengers before his face: and they went, and entered into a village of the Samaritans, to make ready for him. And they did not receive him, because his face was as though he would go to Jerusalem. And when his disciples James and John saw this, they said, Lord, wilt thou that we command fire to come down from heaven, and consume them, even as Elias did? But he turned, and rebuked them, and said, Ye know not what manner of spirit ye are of. For the Son of man is not come to destroy men's lives, but to save them. And they went to another village.*
>
> —Luke 9:52–56 KJV

The scriptural account the disciples were referencing and on which they were basing their proposed plan to Jesus was 2 Kings 1:9–10 (KJV):

> *Then the king sent unto him a captain of fifty with his fifty. And he went up to him: and, behold, he sat on the top of an hill. And he spake unto him, Thou man of God, the king hath said, Come down. And Elijah answered and said to the captain of fifty, If I be a man of God, then let fire come down from heaven, and consume thee and thy fifty. And there came down fire from heaven, and consumed him and his fifty.*

The disciples had chapter and verse, straight from the Bible. That was all they needed, right? Scripture is certainly essential, but it must be interpreted in line with Jesus, who He is, and what He has done for us. The disciples wanted to call fire down from heaven to judge the Samaritans for rejecting the Gospel, just like Elijah did against the enemies of God in the Old Testament. Jesus rebuked them, saying:

> ***Ye know not what manner of spirit ye are of****. For the Son of man is not come to destroy men's lives, but to save them.*
>
> —Luke 9:55–56 KJV, emphasis mine

Jesus was the model and method of ministry, not Elijah. Elijah was considered the chief of the Old Testament prophets. He never even died but was translated, like Enoch, up into heaven. God prophesied in the book of Malachi that Elijah would return, sent by God to call for a revival of the families of Israel before God's final judgment was executed. Elijah was truly remarkable, but when Jesus came, all Scripture had to be configured to Him and not the other way around. Even though the Bible recorded the fire-consuming events in Elijah's day as a positive example of God protecting and affirming the office Elijah held, it could not be called upon as a roadmap of God's will for the disciples. They could only look to Jesus and Him alone. They had to disregard that example and put it in its proper light, the light of Christ. If they had applied Scripture out of the context of Jesus and His ministry (making Elisha the "chief cornerstone" of their belief system), they would have acted in a way God would not have honored. Ultimately Jesus rebuked them.

All Scripture is truth and has great application of truth, but only in the revelation of Jesus. Men and women lose their way when they take their eyes off Jesus. He is the Light! We must apply the Light as we read, and we will see clearly what has been truly said in God's Word.

Moses is the other side of the coin. He was the lawgiver of Israel and ultimately the original author of Scripture. He wrote the first books of the Bible. He penned the words, "In the beginning, God created the heavens and the earth." You cannot get any more original than Genesis 1:1! God called Moses and elevated him as one of the greatest men in the world to ever speak for God. But when Jesus spoke, even Moses' words were 100 percent intended to line up with the revelation of Jesus.

> *For the law was given by Moses, but grace and truth came by Jesus Christ.*
>
> —John 1:17 KJV

There was a great contrast between Moses and Jesus. It is not that Moses wrote untruths, but the words he wrote were only a part and could only reveal so much. Jesus, though, brought the whole truth. He revealed reality, because He is the reality of all that God is. The law of God was and is the Word of God written down for mankind, but Jesus is the eternal, living Word of God. His existence trumps everything ever written with an unmatched supremacy. The nature of God is revealed in magnificent brilliance through Jesus. When He taught from the Torah of Moses, there was an alignment of Holy Scripture through Jesus that unlocked its purest form of truth. There was a common doctrinal conflict in Jesus' day concerning divorce and marriage.

> *And it came to pass, that when Jesus had finished these sayings, he departed from Galilee, and came into the coasts of Judaea beyond Jordan; and great multitudes followed him; and he healed them there. The Pharisees also came unto him, tempting him,*

and saying unto him, Is it lawful for a man to put away his wife for every cause? And he answered and said unto them, Have ye not read, that he which made them at the beginning made them male and female, and said, For this cause shall a man leave father and mother, and shall cleave to his wife: and they twain shall be one flesh? Wherefore they are no more twain, but one flesh. What therefore God hath joined together, let not man put asunder. They say unto him, Why did Moses then command to give a writing of divorcement, and to put her away? He saith unto them, Moses because of the hardness of your hearts suffered you to put away your wives: but from the beginning it was not so. And I say unto you, Whosoever shall put away his wife, except it be for fornication, and shall marry another, committeth adultery: and whoso marrieth her which is put away doth commit adultery.

—Matthew 19:1–9 KJV

Jesus explained why Moses permitted divorce, but then He balanced the discussion with other Scriptures from the Law of Moses. Finally, Jesus contrasted what Moses said with what He was now saying. Jesus said, "Moses allowed you to divorce in certain situations," but then He spoke with clarifying original authority. He said, in contrast, "But ***I say*** unto you." It was as if Jesus explained it like this: "Moses gave you that allowance because of the hardness of your heart, but now I am going to speak on the subject, and what I say goes." Jesus never contradicted Moses or annulled the Law, but He spoke as someone who authored it and not as someone who had *only* read it. Moses, in the most literal sense, was not the author of the books attributed to his name. He would be better described as the transcriber, or the reporter, of the things he heard from the holy angels of God. Jesus, the Word made flesh, was the Author of all Moses ever wrote down. He came not as One who needed angels to speak God's message to Him. He did not even come as a messenger of God! He *is* God's very message. He is the living, breathing message of God. He is the Word Incarnate.

On another occasion earlier in the same chapter, Luke 9, Jesus called three of His disciples to go on a mountaintop excursion into God's glory. This experience is referred to as the "Mount of Transfiguration." It was in this place that God the Father set some things straight as to who Jesus is and where He stands with reference to the great men of God who authored the holy canon.

> *About eight days after Jesus said this, he took Peter, John and James with him and went up onto a mountain to pray. As he was praying, the appearance of his face changed, and his clothes became as*

bright as a flash of lightning. Two men, Moses and Elijah, appeared in glorious splendor, talking with Jesus. They spoke about his departure, which he was about to bring to fulfillment at Jerusalem. Peter and his companions were very sleepy, but when they became fully awake, they saw his glory and the two men standing with him. As the men were leaving Jesus, Peter said to him, "Master, it is good for us to be here. Let us put up three shelters—one for you, one for Moses and one for Elijah." (He did not know what he was saying.)

While he was speaking, a cloud appeared and covered them, and they were afraid as they entered the cloud. A voice came from the cloud, saying, "This is my Son, whom I have chosen; listen to him." When the voice had spoken, they found that Jesus was alone. The disciples kept this to themselves and did not tell anyone at that time what they had seen.

—Luke 9:28–36 NIV

God had marked Jesus as the only One to whom the disciples were to listen, the only One whom they should honor. Peter wanted to build tabernacles to enshrine the place of this spiritual encounter, a tabernacle each for Jesus, Moses, and Elijah. What a grand idea! (I'm being sarcastic.) This account illustrates a blueprint of how men cut themselves off from knowing God and create religion about Jesus rather than a connection to Jesus. They elevate Scripture, great men of God, and even authentic spiritual experiences to be equal with Jesus, or even above Jesus Himself. It is not that the Scriptures, men or women of God, and spiritual experiences are not from God or beneficial, but when they are lifted higher than Jesus in their lives, the competition creates a perversion of truth. Jesus said, "I am the way, the truth, and the life. No one comes to the Father except through Me" (John 14:6 NKJV). The Jews had the holy Scriptures, but Jesus said they could not find the Father, the truth, the way, or the life through those Scriptures alone. Job learned the difference between living a life knowing about God and living a life having encountered the living God. There is a vast gap between the two. Job said it quite directly in the following verse:

> *I have heard of thee by the hearing of the ear:*
> *But now mine eye seeth thee.*
> *Wherefore I abhor myself, and repent*
> *In dust and ashes.*
>
> —Job 42:5–6 KJV

Job knew of God, but ultimately had had never encountered the reality of God in his life. Men and women look to the Scriptures to study God, and they find themselves locked out of the very truth they seek. The Scriptures are not to be blamed, for they certainly reveal God, but only in light of Jesus.

The Father, in dramatic fashion, demonstrated the supremacy of Christ over Moses and Elijah when He spoke these words:

> *"This is my Son, whom I have chosen; listen to him."*
>
> —Luke 9:35 NIV

And suddenly...there was only...Jesus!

Someone may point out that these scenarios were all pre–New Testament. We are now living in the light of His grace, and He has revealed Himself to us. But the same standard must still be actively applied. All Scripture can only be understood in the light of Christ. Outside of Jesus, there is no "true" truth that can be understood, not even from the Bible. Men have come to very unholy conclusions from God's holy Word because they were not following Jesus but rather their own skewed understanding of the Bible. The apostle Peter stands at the front of the line.

Jesus has just died, been resurrected, shown Himself alive, and visibly ascended to the right hand of God, after commanding Peter and the others to "go into all the world and preach the Gospel to every creature." Peter is filled with the Holy Spirit on the Day of Pentecost and boldly preaches the first public proclamation of the risen Lord. Three thousand souls are saved! The Church is birthed, and Peter, along with the eleven other apostles, are at the head of it all, steering and guiding the ship by the influence of the Holy Spirit. They were fulfilling the "Great Commission," preaching the Gospel in Jerusalem, Judea, and even Samaria, but going to the "whole world" was still a bit of a problem. Gentiles were still Gentiles and therefore not included as far Peter and the early Church were concerned. They were biblically "unclean," but God was about to blow up Peter's (and ultimately the churches') theology and thinking:

> *On the morrow, as they went on their journey, and drew nigh unto the city, Peter went up upon the housetop to pray about the sixth hour: And he became very hungry, and would have eaten: but while they made ready, he fell into a trance, and saw heaven opened, and a certain vessel descending upon him, as it had been a great sheet knit at the four corners, and let down to the earth: Wherein were all manner of fourfooted beasts of the earth, and wild beasts, and creeping things, and fowls of the air. And there came a voice to him, Rise, Peter; kill, and eat. But Peter said, Not so, Lord; for I have never eaten any thing that is common or unclean.*

> *And the voice spake unto him again the second time, What God hath cleansed, that call not thou common. This was done thrice: and the vessel was received up again into heaven.*
>
> —Acts 10:9–16 KJV

Peter rebuked the vision when he said, "Not so, I have never eaten any thing that is common or unclean." He was referring to the teachings of the Old Testament. One of the passages he might have had in mind was Leviticus 20:25–26 (KJV, emphasis mind):

> *Ye shall therefore put difference between* ***clean*** *beasts and* ***unclean****, and between unclean fowls and clean: and ye shall not make your souls abominable by beast, or by fowl, or by any manner of living thing that creepeth on the ground, which I have separated from you as* ***unclean****. And ye shall be* ***holy*** *unto me: for I the LORD am holy,* ***and have severed you from other people****, that ye should be mine.*

Peter had lived his whole life by this dietary standard, following it with as much holy fervor as he followed the command "thou shalt not commit adultery." After all, God had said that to eat such things would "make your souls abominable"! That is heavy language, and Peter was right to take God and His Word seriously, but in light of Christ, the full meaning of what God had intended was brought forward, illuminated by an understanding of God's love for the whole world. Remember, John 3:16 had not been written yet! Peter did not know "God so loved the world..." Before the revelation from the Lord about the Gentiles, the early Church would have written John 3:16 something like this: "For God so loved the Jews (and maybe even the Samaritans, who are part Jewish) that He gave His only begotten Son"! God had instituted the dietary laws of the Old Testament as a very practical way of separating the Jews from the other nations, so they would not be corrupted by their pagan standards. The Scripture in Leviticus 20 states this very principle. Jehovah limited what they could eat because He had "severed you (*them*) from *other* people, that ye (*they*) should be mine (*His*)." Israel's holiness was entirely dependent on this civil and social separation.

For the purposes of clarification, I have condensed Leviticus 20:25–26 (KJV) here to bring out this very clear point in the Scriptures:

> *Ye shall therefore put difference between clean beasts and unclean…which I have separated from you as unclean…. Ye shall be holy unto me: for I… have severed you from other people, that ye should be mine.*

I suggest you read Leviticus 20:25–26 in its entirety. There is a direct parallel between diet restrictions and socializing with Gentile societies. The Jews understood this all too well. It was considered a sin to eat pork or to eat with a Gentile. Both these subjects come up in the New Testament as controversial subjects that required correction.

Peter again struggled with the concept of "clean and unclean."

> *But when Peter was come to Antioch, I withstood him to the face, because he was to be blamed. For before that certain came from James, he did eat with the Gentiles: but when they were come,* ***he withdrew and separated himself****, fearing them which were of the circumcision. And the other Jews dissembled likewise with him; insomuch that Barnabas also was carried away with their dissimulation.* ***But when I saw that they walked not uprightly according to the truth of the gospel****, I said unto Peter before them all, If thou, being a Jew, livest after the manner of Gentiles, and not as do the Jews, why compellest thou the Gentiles to live as do the Jews?*
>
> —Galatians 2:11–14 KJV, emphasis mine

Paul said Peter did not walk "uprightly according to the truth of the gospel." The truth of the Gospel is what brought correction to Peter in both instances; he'd followed a certain Scripture passage his whole life that he now was misapplying in light of the Gospel truth revealed in Christ.

Referring back to the rooftop vision, with all the unclean foods that Peter was commanded by God to kill and eat, Peter was immediately rebuked with these words: "What God hath cleansed, *that* call not thou common." God had cleansed something, for which, under the Old Testament, there was not a cleansing available until Jesus. Neither Peter nor the rest of the Church had ever considered the cleansing the cross had extended to all people. Peter had had Scripture's chapter and verse in correct context, and yet he was completely wrong in New Testament application because he did not subject his interpretation of Scripture to the Lordship of Jesus. By applying Scripture without considering first the "cleansing" of God, he was completely wrong in his theology.

Let's not judge Peter too quickly or harshly. Peter represents us all. He represents the Church. We have all looked at the Scriptures without considering the "cleansing" of God. Without that perspective, we will fall into the wrong understanding of what God has said and what He meant. Job is one of the biggest pitfalls theologically. Jesus must be

Lord of the book of Job if we are ever to enjoy the transforming truths embedded in its sacred pages.

Ultimately Peter did get it right. What did he do with all those verses in Leviticus? Did they become obsolete because of the cross? Did Peter just ignore them when reading the Scriptures? With a wave of his hand, did Peter dismiss the Old Testament laws as having no direct application to a New Testament Christian's life? The answer is unequivocally *no*.

> *Therefore, prepare your minds for action, keep sober in spirit, fix your hope completely on the grace to be brought to you at the revelation of Jesus Christ. As obedient children, do not be conformed to the former lusts which were yours in your ignorance, but* ***like the Holy One who called you, be holy yourselves also in all your behavior****; because it is written, "You shall be holy, for I am holy."*
>
> —1 Peter 1:13–16 NASB, emphasis mine

The Scripture from which Peter is quoting is straight out of the book of Leviticus. It is found multiple times in the Bible, but one of these places is in Leviticus 20, where God is giving instructions on clean and unclean foods. Jesus now becomes the center of this revelation found in Leviticus. The command for us to be holy was given in light of the One who is holy, namely God. Now Peter points to God and

His character as the guiding force behind what this verse is stating. God's holiness is demonstrated in His actions and His revealed nature, which guides those actions. Those verses in Leviticus blossom in full display of the actual message, which had nothing to do with eating pork or hanging out with certain people. The message was about following God and imitating his holy character, which is ultimately fulfilled through love. Love is what compelled Jesus to come to the earth and die on the cross to redeem all mankind, the Jew first and also the Gentile. Oddly enough, the command to be holy could only be fulfilled by Peter by going to the Gentiles, eating with them, and sharing the Good News about Jesus!

If Peter could get it wrong, this should give us pause to consider we might be getting it wrong as well. Jesus is our only hope!

Chapter 3

Why Is Satan in Heaven?

Man's plight is one of negative mysteries. A universal question asked by all civilizations is "Why do the righteous suffer?" Religions throughout the history of humanity have been tasked or have tasked themselves with this "unanswerable" challenge. The disciples of Jesus asked a question that rang true with this familiar inquiry:

> *And his disciples asked him, saying, Rabbi, who sinned, this man, or his parents, that he should be born blind?*
>
> —John 9:2 ASV

Accusation and implication oozed out of their question. They assumed so much about what they did not understand. Still, what they asked demands an answer.

Jesus answered, Neither did this man sin, nor his parents.

—John 9:3 ASV

Mankind always has linked tragedy with transgression. The Jewish thought was that if good things are happening to you, you have pleased God, but if evil is attacking, there must be some moral evil in your behavior or thoughts that has opened the door to the assault. Jesus' answer challenged that popular notion, but it also leads us to the original question: "Why *do* the righteous suffer?"

Philosophers and theologians have searched sacred writings and secular theory to bring a cohesive logic to that question. In the search for answers, Job has become for many the obvious "how to" manual for unexplained suffering. The formula goes something like this:

1. *Job was righteous.*

2. *God allowed Job to suffer under the tortures of Satan with no explanation.*

   Conclusion: God has a higher, unexplained reason for the suffering of the righteous.

The answer for many is that there is no answer except that God is the ultimate overseer, so we can conclude there is some "mysterious" good because God has allowed it. Job then becomes nothing more than an empty explanation. It is the God-version of "none of your business!" You may never know the meaning of the loss, but you can be comforted in the idea that there was a meaning. It is a circular argument: The meaning of the suffering is that the suffering has meaning! Around and around it goes! Running faster and faster on this philosophical treadmill leads to a sense of closure without any reality. It is a way to numb the pain while the infection is allowed to eat away the flesh. Everything feels better! "Rejoice, you are not free! Your bondage is actually good!" the devil whispers in your ear. Beware of a message that leaves you in the dark. God is a God of light. He is not the author of confusion.

I remember a time when I received terrible news about one of our church members in the middle of a church service. This church member had just died in a terrible auto accident; she was a young Christian woman at a very young age. I remember being grieved at the situation. She left behind her husband and her children, broken at the loss of this dear mother and wife. I wanted to speak an encouraging word to the people in that church service; it had to be equal parts true, comforting, and sensitive to the people in the congregation who knew her personally. I searched inside my heart for guidance from the Holy Spirit, and He gave me this:

"I know two things are true;

1. This person is in heaven.

2. It was not God's will for her to die."

The person who had died was a faithful Christian who had a relationship with Jesus, and it was evident and fruitful. I knew she had gone to heaven, and that was a source of comfort. The second fact was that I knew it was not God's will for her to have left this world so soon. She was too young, and the Bible makes it clear that God has promised to "satisfy us with long life"! Death is not the friend of God, nor is it your companion either because you are saved. Death is the last enemy. When I made that statement (*"It was not God's will for her to die"*), many were comforted and agreed, but there was one family in the church service that evening who was not related to the person who had died, but they became so offended at such a simple biblical truth. They were upset that anyone would consider a death (and, I assume, any other tragedy) as going against God's will. They believed everything that happened was God's will. How terrible that so many well-meaning Christians have embraced something that leaves God as the ultimate willing Source of all the bad things that happen in this world. But wait! The same well-meaning Christians will quickly point out that it is not God who causes it to happen, but that He allows it for His glory and will to be fulfilled. That is where the book of Job enters the conversation as "exhibit A" to indict God as an accessory to the crime. He becomes a participant in everything evil the devil has been up to lately. "Look at Job," they conclude. "He was a righteous man whom God allowed Satan to attack. Satan was permitted to dismantle every good part of his life, short of killing him." This is not what happened at all.

The first question we must answer in order to understand Job is simple, but it carries profound meaning:

Why Is Satan in Heaven?

This seems to be ignored and accepted by most readers of this text. It is accepted as normal for Satan to be among the "sons of God" speaking to God with authority in heaven. There are some things in Job that should raise eyebrows and questions! There is a certain twisted reality that the book of Job zooms in on, like a camera focusing on a specific angle.

> *Now there was a day when the sons of God came to present themselves before the Lord, and Satan came also among them.*
>
> —Job 1:6 KJV

I picture a scene in heaven in which all these ruling angels are standing in a kind of celestial waiting room, and an announcement comes over the intercom, or maybe another angel just enters the waiting room and announces: "God will see all the sons of God now. Right this way!" As all the angels move toward the entrance to meet with God, there is Satan, right in the middle of them, claiming his spot. Where was the outcry? Why was no one calling for archangel security to stop this imposter from trespassing on heavenly property? Where was Michael the archangel bellowing out with authority, "The Lord rebuke you, Satan! Leave these hallowed halls"? No drama, no violence, just another day in heaven's neighborhood? This is not the picture of heaven we see in the book of Revelation:

> *And I John saw the holy city, new Jerusalem, coming down from God out of heaven.... And there shall in no wise enter into it any thing that defileth, neither whatsoever worketh abomination, or maketh a lie: but they which are written in the Lamb's book of life.*
>
> —Revelation 21:2, 27 KJV

The heaven in the book of Revelation is not the heaven of Job. Satan would not dare set foot in such a pure place. Revelation 21 says nothing that "maketh a lie" shall be allowed even to enter. Satan is not allowed. But in the book of Job, Satan is comfortable and quite bold, standing there before God. These verses of Scripture in Job should inspire many questions that demand answers:

- How is this possible?
- Hadn't Satan already been exiled from heaven when, as Lucifer, he led a rebellion to overthrow God and sit on His throne?
- How did he make it back?
- Why is he there, and why doesn't God just remove him?

The Bible says that Satan's power is death.

Forasmuch then as the children are partakers of flesh and blood, he also himself likewise took part of the same; that through death he might destroy ***him that had the power of death, that is, the devil.***

—Hebrews 2:14 KJV, emphasis mine

Another Scripture brings out something about the timeframe in which Job lived and who was king during his lifetime:

Nevertheless ***death reigned from Adam until Moses****, even over them that had not sinned after the* *likeness of Adam's transgression, who is a figure of him that was to come.*

—Romans 5:14 ASV, emphasis mine

The word *reign* in Romans 5:14 is actually a Greek word that describes the reign of a king. Satan is, in fact, a king. Satan was the king who reigned during the time of Job. Satan's power, according to Hebrews 2:14, is death, and Romans 5:14 personifies death as reigning as a prince from the time of Adam until Moses. Satan is the personification of death. He is the spirit of death. Satan was the king of the earth, and his power was death, released on mankind. Adam released it. God told Adam if he ate from that tree, the tree of the knowledge of good and evil, he would die. Adam was warned by God, in a manner of speaking, that death would reign over him and all humanity. Satan ascended to this throne upon Adam's decision to sin. Adam empowered Satan. That is why the Bible says, "Death reigned from Adam"! Adam was the one who authorized Satan to be the supreme ruler of this planet.

Jesus called Satan the "prince of this world":

Hereafter I will not talk much with you: for the ***prince of this world*** *cometh, and hath nothing in me.*

—John 14:30 KJV

Paul called the devil "the prince of the power of the air":

Wherein in time past ye walked according to the course of this world, according to the ***prince of the power of the air****, the spirit that now worketh in the children of disobedience.*

—Ephesians 2:2 KJV, emphasis mine

Also, Paul referred to the devil as the "god of this world":

In whom ***the god of this world*** *hath blinded the minds of them which believe not, lest the light of the glorious gospel of Christ, who is the image of God, should shine unto them.*

—2 Corinthians 4:4 KJV, emphasis mine

Again, Jesus titled the devil the "prince of this world":

Now is the judgment of this world: now shall the ***prince of this world*** *be cast out.*

—John 12:31 KJV, emphasis mine

So, we see that Satan is a king. He operates as the "god of this world." That is not a self-proclaimed title Satan gave to himself. God gave him that title. The Scriptures, inspired by the Holy Spirit, acknowledged his authority in this world. The devil, as a prince, through wickedness, rules and controls this planet.

> *We know that we are from God, and* ***the whole world lies in the power of the evil one****.*
>
> —1 John 5:19 ESV, emphasis mine

Many people see God as controlling all things with a sort of micro-sovereignty. Not everything in the earth is orchestrated by God; rather, everything in our current world is under the control of Satan.

> *The devil led him up to a high place and showed him in an instant all the kingdoms of the world. And he said to him, "****I will give you all their authority and splendor; it has been given to me, and I can give it to anyone I want to.****"*
>
> —Luke 4:5–6 NIV, emphasis mine

Where did Satan get such authority? In the verses in Luke 4, he says he was *given* this authority. Who gave him this authority? Ultimately Adam gave Satan the authority when he submitted to him and ate from the forbidden tree. God had said not to eat that fruit or he would die:

> *And the Lord God commanded the man, saying, "You may surely eat of every tree of the garden, but of the tree of the knowledge of good and evil you*

> *shall not eat, for in the day that you eat of it* ***you shall surely die****.*"
>
> —Genesis 2:16–17 ESV, emphasis mine

Adam invited death into the world when he ate from the tree.

Satan's authority is Adam's authority. Satan said he had been given this authority, but with the giving also came the right to give away the authority. That was Adam's right as well. He had originally been given authority from God, and with that authority, he had the right to give it away...which he, in fact, did—to Satan.

> *Therefore, just as* ***sin came into the world through one man, and death through sin****, and so death spread to all men because all sinned.*
>
> —Romans 5:12 ESV, emphasis mine

Adam not only represented all mankind, but he also ruled over the entire creation. As man goes, so goes creation. Adam subjected and opened everything up to the power of Satan, and Satan's power was death (Heb. 2:14).

So, all creation was captured by the devil. Adam had ruled everything God had created until he gave it all away. Adam made all the things in the earth and even the earth itself subject to Satan. Nature became corrupted with the devil's nature, and now creation eagerly looks for the day when it is set free:

> *For the creation waits with eager longing for the revealing of the sons of God. For* ***the creation was subjected to futility****, not willingly,* ***but because of him who subjected it****, in hope* ***that the creation itself will be set free from its bondage to corruption*** *and obtain the freedom of the glory of the children of God.*
>
> —Romans 8:19–21 ESV, emphasis mine

Man was meant to be the king of God's creation. God had created everything man needed to reign over it. God had created Adam to be a son of God, to be His image in the earth; that image is a royal image, made just like the King of kings. The psalmist spoke so eloquently about this authority, this special being called man:

> *What is man that you are mindful of him, and the son of man that you care for him? Yet you have made him a little lower than the heavenly beings and crowned him with glory and honor. You have given him dominion over the works of your hands; you have put all things under his feet.*
>
> —Psalm 8:4–6 ESV

God actually gave the earth to man. It does not belong to God presently in the sense that He is controlling it. It was man's property until man gave it away.

> *The heaven, even the heavens, are the* L*ORD's:*
> *But the earth hath he given to the children of men.*
>
> —Psalm 115:16 KJV

We were made to be kings over God's creation, but Adam gave all of his authority to Satan, and Satan took man's place as the prince over it all. Death truly reigned from Adam to Moses.

This is how Satan came to have a place in heaven. This is how Satan came to be regarded as one of the "sons of God." Heaven and earth have always been connected. The Bible is full of examples of the symbiotic relationship between the heavenly and earthly realms.

Jesus taught us to pray:

> *Thy kingdom come. Thy will be done in earth, as it is in heaven.*
>
> —Matthew 6:10 KJV

Jesus taught and demonstrated that whatever heaven is experiencing is legally and literally to happen on the earth.

He called for people to pray in that direction and with that in mind.

> *And I will give unto thee the keys of the kingdom of heaven: and* ***whatsoever thou shalt bind on earth shall be bound in heaven: and whatsoever thou shalt loose on earth shall be loosed in heaven****.*
>
> —Matthew 6:19, KJV, emphasis mine

Again, Jesus taught that there was an unbreakable relationship, a metaphysical bridge, between these two worlds. Within this connection between heaven and earth, there is no way to affect one sphere without affecting the other. What happens in the earth affects heaven, and what happens in heaven affects the earth.

Adam was called a "son of God." He had a place called the Garden of Eden, where heaven and earth met. God Himself went there to meet and fellowship with man. There was no divide between the two. Man was called to rule the earth, and he would do so through his access to God in heaven. Man had authority in heaven and in the earth. When the devil lured Adam and Eve into sin, he took Adam's place as the emperor over creation. He had Adam's earth, and he possessed Adam's place in heaven. Adam had fallen, and Satan was exalted.

Some things got twisted after the fall of Adam and the exaltation of Satan. Before the fall, Satan had no power. He was a fallen angel who had led a failed rebellion against God and had been confined to the earth as a serpent-servant. Adam was a son of God, created to rule over all things, including Satan. Satan, when he tempted Adam and Eve, appeared as a snake. This is significant because Adam and Eve had power over all of God's creation, including the animals.

> *Thou makest him to have dominion over the works*
> *of thy hands; Thou hast put all things under his feet:*
> *All sheep and oxen, Yea, and the beasts of the field,*
> *The birds of the heavens, and the fish of the sea,*
> *Whatsoever passeth through the paths of the seas.*
>
> —Psalm 8:6–8 ASV

Satan appeared to Adam and Eve in a "submitted" form. He came before Adam as a serpent, a form over which Adam ruled. Satan had no power or authority in that garden. Adam could have crushed the head of the serpent right then and there, but instead he chose to abdicate his own throne and chase Eve into rebellion against God!

Adam was a son of God!

> *The son of Enos, the son of Seth, the son of Adam, the son of God.*
>
> —Luke 3:38 ASV

Adam was as much a son of God as Seth was a son of Adam. God used the same words to speak of Adam's sonship as were spoken of Seth's place as Adam's offspring. Adam was a son of God, and Satan was the submitted one, a mere servant under the authority of Adam, but in Job everything was twisted backward. Satan was called as among the sons of God (Job 1:6), and Job was referred to as a mere servant (Job 1:8). There was an exchange between the devil and Adam. They switched places in the universe, and Satan rose to power, all the way to heaven, as Adam fell from the very place God had made for him.

> *And there was war in heaven: Michael and his angels fought against the dragon; and the dragon fought and his angels, and prevailed not;* ***neither was their place found any more in heaven****.*
>
> —Revelation 12:7–8 KJV, emphasis mine

The Scripture says that Satan and his angels had "a place" in heaven. Satan accused man day and night before the throne of God. Humanity had become the slaves of unrighteousness, and Satan was not just their master, but their father. Man, made in the image of God, was reborn with that serpentine nature called sin and death.

Also, Satan had access to the presence of God. This is hard to understand, but it is obvious from the Scripture in Job:

> *And the* L*ORD said unto Satan, Behold, all that he hath is in thy power; only upon himself put not forth thine hand.* ***So Satan went forth from the presence of the* LORD.**
>
> —Job 1:12, KJV, emphasis mine

This was a right reserved for Adam and Eve before the fall. They had access to the presence of God, but they lost it when they sinned. They were driven out from the garden of Eden.

> *And they heard the voice of the* L*ORD God walking in the garden in the cool of the day: and* ***Adam and his wife hid themselves from the presence of the* LORD *God*** *amongst the trees of the garden.*
>
> —Genesis 3:8, KJV, emphasis mine

God was coming to the garden like He always had done, to walk with His kids and enjoy their fellowship. Adam and Eve normally would have run toward His presence, but now there was a separation. They hid in shame, like children caught in their misdeeds. While this was happening, Satan was rising—up, up, up into a place of newly acquired power. Part of that power was access to God! Satan had access to the presence of God, and that gave him power in heaven and earth.

Satan had been given a place of authority in heaven as a king. He had access to the presence of God and spoke for his loyal subjects; Satan was now representing mankind to God! God had to respect this authority Satan possessed because it had ultimately come from God. Like man had previously had, Satan now had authority in these two worlds. He had authority in heaven and in earth.

As the book of Job unfolds, this truth is central to understanding what happens between God and Satan. If you think Satan was just a "nothing" in Job, it is easy to come to the wrong conclusion, that God somehow is the instigator of Job's sufferings.

Many people point to the verse in Job where God and Satan first converse about Job:

> *And the* L*ORD said unto Satan,* ***Hast thou considered my servant Job****, that there is none like him in the earth, a perfect and an upright man, one that feareth God, and escheweth evil?*
>
> —Job 1:8 KJV, emphasis mine

Some people believe God appears to be the instigator of Job's trials. It is often thought of or taught in such a way that Satan would have left Job alone until God said something. To these people, God was prodding Satan to attack Job, and maybe, just maybe, God thinks enough of us, as well, to send Satan as an attack dog after us to destroy our lives as a program of "divine refinement," all for God's glory! How ridiculous! How small God must be to some people, that the only way He can receive glory is to torture His creation, especially the ones who are the most loyal to Him. These well-meaning Christians serve a sadistic idol they call God, but in reality, their god sounds more like Satan than anyone else.

However, when you understand the position Satan had in the book of Job, great clarity comes as to why the events unfolded the way they did. When you read some translations of the Bible, you might be left with a wrong sense of what was conveyed in the original language of the text, whether that be Greek or Hebrew. Job 1:8 in *Young's Literal Translation* brings out the full flavor of what was really said about Job, from God to Satan:

> *And Jehovah saith unto the Adversary, "**Hast thou set thy heart against My servant Job** because there is none like him in the land, a man perfect and upright, fearing God, and turning aside from evil?"*
>
> —Job 1:8 KJV, emphasis mine

God did not sic the devil against Job, but rather He called out the plan that had already formed in Satan's heart. God was pointing out the irony of the devil's crazy scheme. It was as if God was saying, "Of all the people in the world, you want Job? He is the most righteous man on the planet. Why him?" In His omniscience, God already knew what was percolating in the prince of devils' dark mind. He simply addressed it before Satan said something. Satan already knew Job well. Satan does not know everybody on the planet. He is not all-knowing, nor is he all-powerful. He is very limited, so we cannot assume he would even know whom God was speaking of if he did not already have his sights set on Job. Like the demons in Acts 19:15, who knew Paul and knew Jesus but did not know the seven sons of Sceva, so the devil's knowledge has boundaries.

We can also see from God's second encounter with Satan concerning Job that God uses the same language as He did in Job 1:8 to address what was already in Satan's heart:

> *Then the LORD said to Satan, "Have you* ***considered*** *My servant Job, that there is none like him on the earth, a blameless and upright man, one who fears God and shuns evil? And still he holds fast to his integrity, although you incited Me against him, to destroy him without cause."*
>
> —Job 2:3 NKJV

This was the second meeting between God and Satan concerning Job. God already knew that Satan was aware of who Job was, but again He started the conversation with His "inside information" in mind. God never incited Satan, but rather, He was defending Job and his character in both cases. Job was protected by God with a hedge of angelic escorts assigned to ensure his prosperity and well-being. Satan challenged that hedge, because ultimately Job was on his turf—in his kingdom. Remember, Satan was not asking for permission; he was making a demand based on his authority on the earth as king.

When Satan spoke, he spoke with force in his words. He was not whimpering or wondering what would happen; he was demanding an enforcement of legal precedent. He came to God, not for permission, but for a correction. He had the legal right to Job, and he knew it.

> *"But* ***now, stretch out*** *Your hand and* ***touch all*** *that he has, and he will surely curse You to Your face!"*
>
> —Job 1:11 NKJV, emphasis mine

Listen to the way Satan spoke this "request" to God. It did not sound like a request at all. The words *stretch* and *touch* are in the imperative sense in the Hebrew. These were demanding, even commanding tones that sprung from his lips. The devil said, "Now, stretch out Your hand! Now, touch all that he has, and he will surely curse You to Your face!" This was his authority speaking. This was Satan, as a *"son"* of God, the prince of the world, with a place in heaven for him and his angels to enter the presence of God, speaking and demanding that God stretch out His hand and strike Job! What a shocking picture, indeed.

What did God do at this brazen demand? Surely, He smote Satan right out of heaven! I would love to say that God and Michael, along with Gabriel and the whole host of heaven, began to laugh with holy, sarcastic smiles across their faces as their mocking humor quickly morphed into justified outrage. I would take great joy in telling you that was the last day God had to endure the serpent king slithering around heaven, boasting in his regal array while making demands. What pleasure it would have been to tell you God smote him like lightning straight into the bowels of hell for eternity for his insolence. However, in sharp contrast to my desires and lending itself more to my dismay, God said, in a nutshell, "Okay"! God just went along with it. No fighting, no war, no eternal battle that ended in demonic defeat. Satan had captured Job out of the hands of God's protection. Satan had the *right* to launch this attack against Job for one simple reason: Adam was no longer king; Satan was king, and not even God Himself could violate his jurisdiction. More than that, God Himself even enforced what rightfully belonged to Satan.

Jesus, in the book of Mark, comes across a man tortured by demon possession. There were many demons inside the man—so much so that they called themselves "Legion," which is technically a term used to represent six thousand soldiers in a Roman military unit. We do not know how many devils resided in this man, but we do know it was probably in the thousands! Jesus commands the demons to come out! Before exiting, a negotiation ensues between Jesus and a demonic spokesman for the other devils inside. Listen to this conversation and the appeal of the devils:

> *And cried with a loud voice, and said, What have I to do with thee, Jesus, thou Son of the most high God?* ***I adjure thee by God****, that thou torment me not. For he said unto him, Come out of the man, thou unclean spirit.*
>
> —Mark 5:7–8 KJV, emphasis mine

The demons appealed unto God Himself! This is preposterous nonsense, isn't it? I mean, why would devils basically run and hide behind God for protection? When the devil said, "I adjure thee by God," he was claiming legal protection by God Himself. *Matthew Henry's Commentary* brings out the full flavor of what the demons meant in that plea:

> He deprecates his wrath; I *adjure thee*, that is, "I earnestly beseech thee, by all that is sacred,

> I beg of thee for God's sake, by whose permission I have got possession of this man (*Matthew Henry's Commentary*),

One Greek commentary defines *adjure* as "to give a command to someone under oath, *adjure, implore*."

What made these demons feel so bold as to *command* Jesus? They were used to being in charge. They knew Jesus as the Son of the Most High God, and yet they still attempted to tell Him what to do with His power. They had never been cast out of anyone before. Throughout the Old Testament, many miracles took place. People were healed on many occasions, and deliverance is recorded throughout from Genesis to Malachi. The Red Sea is parted, and the walls of Jericho were shouted down. Armies fell before Israel in spectacular fashion with the backing of God's power. Even resurrections are recorded on multiple occasions in the Old Testament. The only thing oddly left out was that not one saint or prophet or priest ever cast a demon out of a person. The only way to dislodge a demon from a human was to kill the person. No one, not even Israel, had authority over demons. For four thousand years, the dark forces of the devil were running the show.

What shock and awe must have ensued when the devils realized—for the first time since Adam—that man had authority over them again. These devils knew God, in His righteousness, had to enforce their legal right to rule in the earth. Satan had power in heaven and in the earth. In Job 1, we see Satan commanding God, and in Mark 5 we see demons in the earth commanding Jesus.

Someone may say, "Yes, the devil spoke to God in commanding tones, but God did not have to listen to him!" God must do what is right even if it leads to evil. God gave mankind the power to sow whatever he would like to grow in the earth through the power of seed. Man sows it, and God grows it. Man chooses the crop, and God has supplied the soil, sunlight, and rain. God and His Word have created all these processes, and God holds them all together so they always work. Man plants apple seeds and grows apple trees. The process will work. Man can plant tomatoes, and they will grow if all necessary ingredients are supplied. This process works time and time again because God is backing it up. These scientific laws were put in place by God. So, what if man decides to grow plants for the purpose of using the plants as drugs to destroy young people's lives? Is that evil to grow plants that kill and destroy? Yes! Does God step into the process and stop it because it is evil? No! Man has that authority on the earth, and God will not only not step in to interfere, but when all of the ingredients that are needed to grow those marijuana or poppy plants are met, He will still enforce the process with His scientific laws. God gave that power to man, and it would be unjust to renege on the covenant because of the consequential evil, which God abhors. Is God in favor of destroying lives? Of course not! Will God judge mankind for these abuses of power? Of course! But God will not go back on His Word. He will enforce the terms of His agreements. The same is true for the power Satan has secured. God is under His own righteous obligation to abide by and enforce legal authorizations, even on behalf of the devil.

Look at Job 2:3, and you will find some of the most disturbing words ever spoken by God about how far-reaching was this authority of the devil:

> *And the LORD said unto Satan, Hast thou considered my servant Job, that there is none like him in the earth, a perfect and an upright man, one that feareth God, and escheweth evil? and still he holdeth fast his integrity, although* ***thou movedst me against him, to destroy him without cause****.*
>
> —Job 2:3 KJV, emphasis mine

The Lord states that Satan moved Him. *Satan moved God!* Let that settle in your imagination for a moment. As crazy as the idea is that God could be moved by the devil, the next thing God says will truly stretch your mind: *All of this was done for no reason*. God Himself says there was no cause. Satan not only could move God, but he did not have any reason to be able to move God when he moved God! The next six different translations of Job 2:3 will bring out the gravity of God's statement:

> *Although you incited me against him to destroy him* ***without reason****.*
>
> —Job 2:3 ESV, emphasis mine

> ***You caused me*** *to ruin him* ***for no good reason****, but he continues to be without blame.*
>
> —Job 2:3 NCV, emphasis mine

> *"****You wanted*** *me to destroy him* ***without any reason****. But he still continues to be faithful."*
>
> —Job 2:3 NIRV

> *And he still maintains his integrity, though* ***you incited me*** *against him to ruin him* ***without any reason****.*
>
> —Job 2:3 NIV

> *He still holds fast his integrity, although* ***you moved me*** *against him, to destroy him* ***without cause****.*
>
> —Job 2:3 RSV, emphasis mine

> *And still he is keeping hold on his integrity, and* ***thou dost move Me*** *against him to swallow him up* ***for nought!***
>
> —Job 2:3 YLT, emphasis mine

What an amazing picture of how absolute the authority was that Satan received from Adam! An unusually oxymoronic picture of the sheer force of Adam's authority with God is seen in this interaction between Satan and God. Adam could have asked for anything on earth, and it would have been his for the taking. He forfeited this power over to the devil, and the result was a catastrophe with limitless consequences.

All this information would be very negative and depressing if that's where it stopped. The Gospel is Good News, so thank God there is more to the story!

Chapter 4

Christ Strikes Back

God's dilemma goes something like this: How does a holy God, who cannot lie, redeem a sinful humanity who is owned rightfully by a master to whom mankind willfully sold itself in defiance of the God who sacrificially loves them? The problem with Satan was that he now had legal claim over humanity. He did not win this prize unlawfully. Quite the contrary, he used the rules, set up by God, artfully to gain his royal advantage and prestige. Job is the perfect picture of this dilemma.

The book of Job was written as an inspired dissertation of mankind under Satan's reign. As I shared earlier, the name *Job* is believed to mean "fatherless." God included the book of Job in the Bible to illustrate the desperate situation in which human beings found themselves without God as their Father, captured by this "thing" called "the devil." The book of Job shows the impotence of perfection over parentage. Job was the picture of righteousness, but God was not his daddy. God made a very sad statement in Job 1:8, when he referred to Job as "My servant." Some will read that statement and see only a positive word, but at its core was a perversion of the perfect destiny God had planned for mankind, for Job himself. God had meant for him to be His son, not His servant, and no matter how much man served God, it was not going to change this fact: Satan was now man's father and Satan was still the king.

So back to the divine dilemma: What was God to do? Someone may say, "God is omnipotent! The devil was no match for His might!" and they would be right, but the issue was not a question of power, but of righteousness. God can not violate His own righteous nature. He cannot violate His own Word. He is the Word; He is His Word. It would be a form of self-destruction. It is an impossibility for God to do wrong or to do less than His Word. The rules matter. God's rules are eternal standards that God Himself will not violate because they proceed from His nature. So, the big question for God to reverse the curse legally and rightfully is this: What are the rules that even God had to play by to redeem mankind?

Hebrews 2:14 (KJV) states the foundation of the redemption rulebook:

> *Forasmuch then as the children are partakers of flesh and blood, he also himself likewise took part of the same; that through death he might destroy him that had the power of death, that is, the devil.*

Rule 1: Man started it; man had to fix it.

God could not fix this by His omnipotence. In the garden, Satan did not have any power over Adam and Eve to make them eat the fruit of that tree. He simply tempted King Adam through Eve, and Adam through sin submitted his kingdom to darkness. God would have to play by the same rules Satan had played by when he rose to power. The problem started through a man, and therefore God had to fix it through a man. The challenge was that all men were captive to the decision of Adam. There was only one possibility left in the entire universe: God had to become a man. The Word of God would become flesh. The irony is that God's all-powerful word had limited His ability to save man, so God sent His Word as a man, to save man from sin. John 1:14 says "the Word became flesh." That is the amazing miracle of the Incarnation: God became a man. I do not think the devil saw it coming. The devil does not understand the insane limits love will go to in order to reach the loved. God's willingness to become a man was the "zig" when the devil thought God was going to "zag"! Flesh and blood clothed the eternal God...and not just as some sort of anthropomorphic costume. God became man in every way that man is man. Nor was this a temporary situation for the God of heaven and earth. God was committing to humanity for eternity. "Why would something so exalted stoop so low for such limited and weak beings?" This was Satan's thought because he only understands selfish ambition and power. He is unfamiliar with the concept of love and sacrifice. Perfection is what the imperfect one, Satan, seeks, and humans do not meet his standards. God is perfect, but He loves the imperfect and will do anything to save them…even becoming one of them.

> *For since by man came death, by man came also the resurrection of the dead. For as in Adam all die, even so in Christ shall all be made alive.*
>
> —1 Corinthians 15:21–22 KJV

In this passage, Paul states that this rule was put in place due to the original setup in the garden. "For since by man came death" makes it clear that the original fall created a justified symmetry for redeeming mankind. In other words, because a man enthroned death, then man also had to be the one to dethrone death. God could not do it as God. God could only fix this as a man.

Rule 2: Death is the currency of redemption.

God had to destroy death through death! Death was the prescribed payment for Adam's sin. God would enforce this payment with rigid integrity. God told Adam in Genesis that the day in which he ate of the tree of the knowledge of good and evil, he would surely die.

For the wages of sin is death…

—Romans 6:23 KJV

Death is a wage, or as we might say, it is a currency. It is the currency of the kingdom of darkness. It is within the framework of the satanic economy that Jesus would make His transaction complete.

Death took possession of the throne of man, and it would only be through the payment of death that death could be destroyed. Death was king until another king swallowed Death in Himself. As a man, Jesus would only be able to defeat Death by dying the death of the sinner. Jesus had to take our place, become our sin, to die our death!

Rule 3: The "Son of God" clause is in effect.

Adam was a son of God, and that gave him the right to rule creation like God intended. Being a "son of God" is a legal position before God. The phrase "son of God" in the Scriptures is a title of authority. It was often used for those who are members of a certain class. Adam was in the class of God because he was made in God's image, meant to rule like God! He was invested with God's power and command.

After the fall of man into sin, man went from a son of God to a slave. He became a slave to everything. Even the way man related to God was through servanthood alone. Adam gave Satan his jurisdiction, and Adam could only do that because he was a son of God over the earth. God the Father could not come down to the earth and fix this problem. He had to send His own Son. A son of God gave it all away, and it would have to be the Son of God who restored it.

> ***For it is not possible*** *that the blood of bulls and of goats should take away sins. Wherefore when he cometh into the world, he saith, Sacrifice and offering thou wouldest not, but* ***a body hast thou prepared me****.*
>
> —Hebrews 10:4–5 KJV, emphasis mine

The words "it is not possible" indicate that not even God Himself could make it happen by just willing it. God could not use His power to make the blood of bulls and goats take away sins. If He could have, then you can believe He would have done that in a minute versus sending His own Son to become sin and die for us. God had to do it a certain way…a legal way…the righteous way.

One interesting characteristic about God is that His abilities extend as far as His nature and His willingness to act. Where God is unwilling to act, that action is impossible because God only acts according to His nature. Because God's nature is unchanging, the only things that are possible are those actions that are in line with His eternal nature! For example, if God is righteous, then it is an impossibility for God to act unrighteously. It is not just that God will never act unrighteously, but that God is and always has been righteous, so unrighteousness is not one of the options for God to act upon now or ever. It is possible to be sinless, even while it is possible to be tempted to sin. Jesus, as a man, demonstrated this truth through His human nature. God is beyond just being sinless. He is righteous in the sense that He cannot even be tempted. When the Bible says that "it is not possible" for a bull's blood to take away sins, there is an eternal boundary being described concerning God's ability to act. In other words, God is in one sense limited to what and how certain things must be done. It is also worth noting that God is not wanting to do some specific thing but is held back in frustration by some promise made without proper forethought. The reason a thing is impossible for God is because He is unwilling to do it—not in divine stubbornness, but in the unchanging position of His eternal divine nature. It was an impossibility for the blood of animals to take away our sins because God would redeem us rightfully, and bulls and goats are not sufficient. Unless God were a thief, we could only be paid for with proper currency. That currency was a blood and a body with proper value. It had to be of extraordinary worth. After all, God was not redeeming animals, plants, or even angels. He was purchasing beings made in His own image. They were like Him. They were replicas of God almighty. What is the price tag of a son of God? Greater than that, what is the price of all the sons of God? A son of God could only be purchased with another Son of God. There was an exchange that had to take place!

Rule 4: We were redeemed under the Law!

Why did God wait so long to send Jesus? Why didn't He send His Son as one of the first children of Eve? Eve could have carried Emmanuel through immaculate conception, and Cain could have killed Him. Problem solved, right!? Jesus could have resurrected, Adam and Eve could have been saved, and Cain might have been thrown into hell as the only unrepentant sinner! This makes sense on paper. Less time, less mess! But God did not do it that way because it would not have redeemed us. There was a timing ingredient that could not be violated:

> ***But when the fulness of the time was come, God sent forth his Son****, made of a woman, made under the law, to redeem them that were under the law, that we might receive the adoption of sons.*
>
> —Galatians 4:4–5 KJV, emphasis mine

There was a certain timing to our redemption. The Law of God was a mandatory piece of the transaction, necessary to ultimately enforce the coming payment. Remember, Job was blameless, and Death reigned over him just fine. Living right was, by itself, not redemptive nor protective from Adam to Moses. Death reigned over Job and every other saint. Death passed onto all men, even the ones who had not transgressed any law. Death, for the first time, found a boundary at the Law of Moses. There was a line that not even Death could cross called the commandments of God. If God's ordinance was held to, Life was the promise.

> *See, I have set before thee this day* ***life*** *and good, and* ***death*** *and evil; in that I command thee this day to love the* L*ORD* *thy God, to walk in his ways, and to* ***keep his commandments*** *and his statutes and his judgments,* ***that thou mayest live*** *and multiply: and the* L*ORD* *thy God shall bless thee in the land whither thou goest to possess it.*
>
> —Deuteronomy 30:15–16 KJV, emphasis mine

> *I call heaven and earth to record…that I have set before you life and death…therefore choose life, that both thou and thy seed may live.*
>
> —Deuteronomy 30:19 KJV

God called upon heaven and earth to record the eternal proclamation through His Law. The Law defined where Life began and Death ended its reign. There was a separation for the first time since before the fall of man in the garden of Eden. The Law was God's way of limiting the work of Satan in His people's lives. It was perfect, holy, and just...but man was the antithesis of all those things. The Law was made weak through man's flesh. Man's ability to keep the Law was infinitely useless. In fact, his attempt to keep it would enflame his sinful passions to furious burnings. The Law was a weight to a drowning person. It worked against sinful man. There was a perversion that emerged from this union between man's flesh and God's Law, something more horrid than sin itself. This demonic alien thing that came crawling up out of man was called self-righteousness. Sin is bad, and it produces death, but self-righteousness produces murderers—and not just any kind of killers; it creates God-killers. The Law was crucial for Jesus to accomplish His saving mission justifiably. There were two factors the Law produced that would validate our redemption:

1. Jesus was truly worthy by an objective standard of sin and holiness. The Law was needed as a measuring stick of sinlessness. It was the divine holy code of redemption. It was like a lock with an innumerable configuration of possible numbers that all must line

up together to open the code called: HOLY. The holy code was the ultimate legal identifier of the "Lamb of God" that would take away our sins and the sins of the whole world. Jesus was the fulfillment of the Law.

Think not that I am come to destroy the law, or the prophets: I am not come to destroy, but to fulfil.

—Matthew 5:17 KJV

The word *fulfill* is a Greek word that means "to fill up to the fullest." It gives the picture of a jar or vessel filled with water until it can hold no more liquid. The idea is fullness, completion, and accomplishment. Jesus was sent to complete the law code of God for the first time ever. No man was even capable of truly living the Law. But Jesus came and embodied its sacred words perfectly in obedience and grace. Every command was kept by Him in its purest form and intent! He was heir to all its promised blessings of life and goodness! The Law said that if a person kept God's commands, they would have all God's blessings! No sickness, no tragedy, no death! Jesus was measured in every way and found to be the perfectly perfect perfection God required.

For he hath made him to be sin for us, ***who knew no sin****; that we might be made the righteousness of God in him.*

—2 Corinthians 5:21 KJV, emphasis mine

> ***Who did no sin**, neither was guile found in his mouth.*
>
> —1 Peter 2:22 KJV, emphasis mine

> *For we have not an high priest which cannot be touched with the feeling of our infirmities; but was in all points tempted like as we are, **yet without sin**.*
>
> —Hebrews 4:15 KJV, emphasis mine

Jesus did not know sin, commit sin, or give in to sin in any way! He was the spotless Lamb of God! The Law, with its ability to pull out the sinfulness of man from hiding and stir its manifestation into the light, could pull nothing out of Jesus except the purity of God!

> *For as by one man's disobedience many were made sinners, **so by the obedience of one shall many be made righteous**. Moreover the law entered, that the offence might abound. But where sin abounded, grace did much more abound: That as sin hath reigned unto death, even so might grace reign through righteousness unto eternal life by Jesus Christ our Lord.*
>
> —Romans 5:19–21 KJV, emphasis mine

Jesus had to obey where all other men had failed. Jesus was holy in every way that fallen man had no power to be. His obedience was just as redemptive as His dying on the cross! If He had not obeyed the Law, He never could have qualified as our sacrifice. That's why God had to protect Jesus as a baby from being killed by Herod. Jesus could not have died as a baby and redeemed us. He had not obeyed God's Law yet. He had not been tempted in all the ways that we are tempted and fail. That had to happen first for any of it be potent!

Paul said that "the Law entered, that the offense might abound." The Law was given to cause sin to abound. Why would God create such a thing? The Law was the magnifier and multiplier of the nature of whatever was brought under its scrutiny. When a man full of sin attempts to keep the Law, his true nature is revealed to him, to his frustration. Paul spoke about the effect of the Law on fallen man:

> *What shall we say then? Is the law sin? God forbid. Howbeit, I had not known sin, except through the law: for I had not known coveting, except the law had said, Thou shalt not covet: but sin, finding occasion, wrought in me through the commandment all manner of coveting:* ***for apart from the law sin is dead****. And I was alive apart from the law once:* ***but when the commandment came, sin revived,***

> ***and I died****; and the commandment, which was unto life, this I found to be unto death.*
>
> —Romans 7:7–10 ASV, emphasis mine

That is what is so amazing about the man named Jesus. He was born under the Law, but the Law only stirred up righteousness in Christ. His nature was sinless. The Law only revealed the purity in Jesus.

When Paul stated in Romans 7:10 that "the commandment, which was unto Life," he was referring to the original intent of God in giving the Law. The commandment was intended to lead to Life. What kind of life? The eternal Life of God. Jesus secured legally the right, as a man, to eat from the tree from which Adam had been restrained from partaking when he was driven from the garden of Eden. Jesus had access to the Life of God. It is as if a man had been given access to the paradise garden again. The Tree of Life is before Him, and the other tree Adam had eaten from, that crowned death as king, is there as well. Jesus stands before God with the ability to eat from the tree of life and live forever, unable to die.

That is when God flips the script in a way no one could see coming. Love had planned an outrageous ploy! It was a selfless suicide-mission of sorts, both physically and even metaphysically! How could God think up such a thing, much less do it? It was a gruesome strategy with unlimited risk and no safety net. "Oh, the Reckless Love of God" as the song goes! He would slaughter a Lamb…a pure Lamb…the Lamb of God! Jesus was the only man who had the right to live forever, having never known sin, and God was going to ask Him to die by becoming sin. Jesus was to drink of a cup that He hated. How was this to happen? God was commanding Jesus to drink of the very thing that had killed Adam and Eve. This was madness! Jesus was not just a righteous man, but a man who was also God incarnate! This was it. There was no other to take His place or to try again if it failed. God was putting everything on the line to win us. He was giving us His only begotten Son! Jesus was to become sin for us. Sinless Sin! Has anyone ever heard of something so contradictory…or genius? Jesus would have to choose between living forever or becoming the very thing He hated. Where Adam had been commanded to not eat from that tree, Jesus was now being commanded to drink of a cup full of the juices from that same tree. What perplexing irony! Jesus was righteous, and the command of His Father, whom He so loved, was to ingest the very thing He so hated. Love drove the Father's plan, and it was that love that drove His Son to die for us!

2. The second thing the Law produced was the Pharisee! Once again, I will refer to what Paul said in Galatians:

> ***But when the fulness of the time was come, God sent forth his Son****, made of a woman, made under the law, to redeem them that were under the law, that we might receive the adoption of sons.*
>
> —Galatians 4:4–5 KJV, emphasis mine

There was a certain timing to redemption for Christ's sacrifice on the cross to truly save and redeem. This was not some esoteric timing shrouded in divine mystery. Yes, only God knew the timing, but He has revealed in Scripture what was needed and the reasons behind the timing of Jesus' arrival on earth. The Pharisee was an essential part of the crucifixion process. Yes, the Romans invented crucifixion as their own unique model of capital punishment, but the Pharisees were necessary to carry out such punishment on the Son of God.

Who killed Jesus? This has been a debate for over 1,900 years now. The Jews have unjustly been accused as a nation of being guilty of His death. Justin Martyr, an early second-century Church father, reiterated as much in *Dialogue of Justin with Trypho, a Jew* when he explained the reasoning for the Jews' hardships, like their exile and their loss of the temple. He declared, "Accordingly, these things have happened to you in fairness and justice, for you have slain the Just One, and His prophets before Him." Many Church fathers have echoed these same simplistic conclusions. Though some Jews were involved in the crucifixion, many were against it, including Jesus' own mother, Mary.

Some have said it was the Jews and Gentiles alike who participated to slay the Messiah, and there is some truth to that statement.

> *Who by the mouth of thy servant David hast said, Why did the heathen rage, and the people imagine vain things? The kings of the earth stood up, and the rulers were gathered together against the Lord, and against his Christ. For of a truth against thy holy child Jesus, whom thou hast anointed, both* ***Herod****, and* ***Pontius Pilate****, with the* ***Gentiles****, and* ***the people of Israel****, were gathered together, for to do whatsoever thy hand and thy counsel determined before to be done.*
>
> —Acts 4:25–28 KJV, emphasis mine

The early Church prayed this verse from Psalm 2:1–2 to God as a prophetic foretelling of the crucifixion of Jesus. In this verse, all peoples were represented, and their local leaders, as having participated in and being guilty of the killing of the Lord!

Still different groups, in a representative sense, point out that it was humanity's sin that drove the nails into His hands and feet. "Everyone is guilty of the death of Jesus" is often stated, because we have all sinned, and our sins were ultimately what drove Jesus to the cross. Once again, I would agree with that conclusion.

By themselves, the Romans and the Jews would have left Jesus alone. Many Jews and Gentiles alike believed in and honored Jesus as the Son of God! Rather, it was a special breed of evil that planned and instigated the supreme murder of the Messiah! The Law was the standard by which all righteousness is measured. Because of this, we can see how the Law of God validated Jesus as the Lamb of God. But the Law had another purpose that would help make the Passion possible. To steal, you need a thief. To betray, you need a betrayer. To deceive, you need a liar, and to kill the Son of God, you would need a Pharisee. The Pharisee is the most unlikely of characters to be involved in the most vicious of crimes. The Pharisees were a sect that likely evolved out of the desire among dedicated Jews to keep God's laws with all available effort. It was a resistance movement against the pagan cultures to which the Jews had been exposed during their captivities. The Pharisees were a counterculture movement intended to preserve the keeping of the Law as the cornerstone of the Jewish people. They dedicated themselves in extreme discipline to obey the Law in every part of their lives.

The *Lexham Bible Dictionary* describes the Pharisees' origin and purpose:

> **Pharisees** (Φαρισαῖος, *Pharisaios*). Members of a Jewish party that exercised strict piety according to Mosaic law. The Pharisees were a sect within early Judaism, becoming active around 150 BC and enduring as a distinct party until being subsumed into the Rabbinic movement around AD 135.

It is interesting to note that the Pharisees came about and developed as a group 150 years before Jesus was born, and they died off as a group about one hundred years after Jesus' death. It is as if the Pharisees' purpose was to participate in the crux of history. They seem to be the group that was made for that cursed hour of Christ's death. To understand the Pharisaic function in redemption, you must understand what opposition to righteousness looks like. The opposite of righteousness is not sin; it is self-righteousness. Sinners loved Jesus because Jesus was "made" for them. In other words, Jesus is a Savior to sinners. He was born to do that very thing. Sinners were drawn to the Master, and they followed Him because He had what they needed; He *was* the thing they needed. The sinner came thirsty, and Jesus said, "I am the water of life." But self-righteousness is, at its core, anti-righteousness. It stands against everything God loves while also striving to serve God and imitate His holy nature. It is the original fruit that hung from the tree that killed Adam and Eve. God's strongest language is reserved for His description and disgust of self-righteousness:

> *But we are all as an unclean thing,*
> *And all our righteousnesses are as filthy rags.*
>
> —Isaiah 64:6 KJV

Notes for the NET Bible (Isaiah 64:6) state:

> *Heb* "and like a garment of menstruation [are] all our righteous acts"; KJV, NIV "filthy rags"; ASV "a polluted garment."

The Bible calls self-righteousness akin to a used garment that a woman might wear during her menstrual period. It the picture of a useless, defiled thing. It is a garment that represents fruitlessness. That is a righteousness that is self-generated.

Paul describes, in the strongest of terms, the contrast between self-righteousness and that righteousness that Christ gives:

> *Circumcised the eighth day, of the stock of Israel, of the tribe of Benjamin, an Hebrew of the Hebrews; as touching the law, a Pharisee; concerning zeal, persecuting the church; touching the righteousness*

> *which is in the law, blameless…and do count them but dung, that I may win Christ.*
>
> —Philippians 3:5–8 KJV

Paul referred to himself as a Pharisee, and yet he categorized his self-energized efforts to follow the Law of God as "dung." The *Message* uses even stronger language:

> *You know my pedigree: a legitimate birth, circumcised on the eighth day; an Israelite from the elite tribe of Benjamin; a strict and devout adherent to God's law; a fiery defender of the purity of my religion, even to the point of persecuting the church; a meticulous observer of everything set down in God's law Book….*
>
> *Yes, all the things I once thought were so important are gone from my life. Compared to the high privilege of knowing Christ Jesus as my Master, firsthand, everything I once thought I had going for me is insignificant—dog dung. I've dumped it all in the trash so that I could embrace Christ and be embraced by him. I didn't want some petty, inferior brand of righteousness that comes from keeping a list of rules when I could get the robust kind that comes from trusting Christ—God's righteousness.*
>
> —Philippians 3:5–9 MSG

Jesus is everything man was meant to be when man is connected to God and God's righteousness. The Pharisee is the complete opposite. The Pharisee is what man becomes at the climax of his self-effort to be right before God. Man, disconnected from God, willing himself to be good, stimulates certain self-righteous elements in his nature that drive him to kill anything truly like God. God's righteousness is juxtaposed to man's righteousness when Jesus is contrasted with the Pharisee. You see a paradoxical similarity polarized infinitely between the Pharisee striving to keep the Law and Jesus truly fulfilling the Law. Though Jesus and the Pharisee could be said to both be pursuing God through obedience to His commandments, they are such opposing products of the very Law they are keeping. Jesus is the Lamb according to the Law, and the Pharisee, in his zeal for the Law, murders the Lamb of God. Only the Law could reveal the brightness of Jesus and the darkness of the Pharisees at the same time. Only the Law could qualify Jesus to die for us and produce a humanity so wretched, it would facilitate His death. It was not the greatest sinners who were motivated to crucify Jesus, but the greatest followers of the Law of God.

Chapter 5

War in Heaven

Every war throughout history has been a consummation of multiple battles that have led up to a decisive battle that determined the final outcome and ultimately the victor. Whether we look to the now-famous battle known as the Siege of Orleans, in which Joan of Arc helped save her people from English rule, or the Siege of Yorktown, in 1781, that ultimately decided the result of the Revolutionary War and America's fate, we can see example after example of a final strategic blow that finalized the winners and losers of these grand conflicts. The greatest war ever waged was fought not for land or even humanity's earthly freedoms, but it was eternal in its consequences. This war had several battles, and ultimately a final, violent engagement that was the deathblow to establish a clear and permanent champion. Jesus describes where this campaign started:

And from the days of John the Baptist until now the kingdom of heaven suffereth violence, and the violent take it by force.

—Matthew 11:12 KJV

Another translation adds more detail:

But <from the days of John the Immerser, until even now> The kingdom of the heavens [is being invaded], And [invaders] are [[seizing upon it]].

—Matthew 11:12 EMPH

John the Baptist was born six months before Jesus was born, to make a straight path for the Savior to execute His assignment. John had a mission upon his life even in the womb of Elizabeth. He was created to proclaim the coming of the Lord. He was the greatest of the prophets, and the beginning of his life and ministry was the start of the heavenly struggle. This war would not end until the final blow was inflicted by Jesus, when He walked through heaven's gates, victorious over death. Satan and his cohorts had never truly suffered defeat until John and Jesus showed up on the earth. They had seen a few setbacks concerning Israel, but the Roman empire seemed to have that under control by the time John and Jesus were born. God had failed His people, at least in Satan's mind. He had everything within his scaly grip, and Jehovah seemed to be losing ground at every turn in the road of time—but that's when there was a sudden divine pivot! God brought the *J* team on the scene. It might have looked like a normal birth—just another son of Abraham born into captivity—but it was the blowing of the trumpet in Zion. It was a call to arms. John was to be the consummation of the prophets of the Old Testament, and Jesus was to bring in a new wine never before drunk by the lips of men. John came declaring the Lord's coming, riding through Israel like Paul Revere, but unlike Mr. Revere, Paul was heralding a message from God Himself. The armies of the demonic knew something was amiss. There was a frightful stirring in that dark camp as the orc-like creatures of the damned writhed in hopeless anticipation. Suddenly and without any alert, legions of warring angels were marching boldly through Israel's skies. Innumerable soldiers of light pierced across the night air to declare that a war had begun.

> *And there were shepherds.... And the angel said to them, Stop being afraid. For behold, I am bringing you good tidings of great joy.... And suddenly there was with the angel* ***a multitude of the army of heaven****, praising God and saying, Glory in the highest places to God, and upon earth peace among men of good will.*
>
> —Luke 2:8–14 WUEST, emphasis mine

Why did God send an army of angels to announce the birth of His Son? When Jesus was born, there was violence on the earth, and there was fighting in heaven. A battle had begun, and I believe Jesus dealt the first blow simply in His birth. Jesus was the invasion of heaven into the earth.

The second defeat of the devil came in the ministry of Jesus. Jesus declared in Luke 10:18–19 (NKJV):

> *And He said to them, "I saw Satan fall like lightning from heaven."*

Many have thought this Scripture was talking about the original fall of Lucifer in Isaiah 14 and Ezekiel 28. That couldn't be further from the truth. Jesus was describing Satan's fall after creation.

The devil was defeated in a big way the day Jesus was triumphant over him in the temptations in the wilderness. He fell that day. He lost something in heaven. It was not the permanent defeat that would come later through Jesus' blood shed on the cross and the subsequent resurrection, but Satan had been personally defeated. As far as Jesus was concerned, it was as if Satan had been crushed already and removed from heaven, even before Jesus' death on the cross. Why was Jesus able to do this? Jesus had done something no man had ever accomplished: He had lived a sinless life!

> *Hereafter I will not talk much with you: for* ***the prince of this world*** *cometh, and* ***hath nothing in me****.*
>
> —John 14:30 KJV, emphasis mine

Satan had nothing in Him. There was no place for the devil in His life. No accusations, no condemnation, no judgment—just unadulterated righteousness! Satan could not stand against this Man. Because he had no place in Jesus, he had no place in heaven to speak against Him to the Father. Jesus operated as King over creation while here on this earth. Satan had ruled for so long with little resistance, but now this Nazarene had flicked him aside like he was nothing. Heaven was alive with discord. Every man had his weakness, and there was nothing to stop the demonic hoards so long as there was sin somewhere lurking in the dark DNA of mankind. It was different with Jesus, though. It was not just that He was keeping all the rules, but that He was truly righteous from His heart! He was pure light radiating, even cutting like a laser through the tangible darkness with the ease of a hot blade through newly churned butter. He was unlimited, and Satan was a wisp of ash before him. There was war in heaven because there was a Man now on earth who could not be touched with sin. The angels of God drove Satan out of his place, and he found himself with the wind flowing through his stringy mop of hair; falling, plunging, descending unwillingly to the earth. You can almost hear the *crack* of the earth as he thudded upon the ground. Shaken and disoriented from the extreme force by which he had been pushed into the earth, he crawled out of the crater still smoldering from his collision—defeated...by...a...*man?*!

> *And He said to them, "**I saw Satan fall like lightning from heaven**. Behold, I give you the authority to trample on serpents and scorpions, and over all the power of the enemy, and nothing shall by any means hurt you."*
>
> —Luke 10:18–19 NKJV, emphasis mine

Jesus turned to the disciples and empowered them over all the power of the enemy. So long as they operated in His name, they would walk in the same victory Jesus had secured through His sinless life. They were operating with His righteousness credited to their account. They could act just like they were sinless men because they followed Jesus and He had that power over the devil. He had that power, not because He was God, but because He was a truly righteous Man. This power belonged to Jesus, and He could give it to any man who believed in Him.

Most believe Lucifer fell so long ago—before man was even created. But the fall Jesus spoke of in Luke 10 was not about that pre-creation fall, but rather a fall that would allow

Him to authorize the disciples to trample on serpents and scorpions. Lucifer fell from heaven long ago, but that fall from heaven never gave man any power over the devil. Adam and Eve, before they sinned in the garden, had had power over him. They could have cast him out of the garden, but instead they listened and gave in to his offer. No other man since Adam could trample on or have power over the enemy until Jesus came and Satan fell once again. No prophet or saint had ever cast out a devil in the Old Testament. They had raised the dead and healed the sick. They had even seen great signs and wonders at the hands of men of God, but no one man, no matter how holy or anointed, could touch a devil until Jesus defeated Satan in the wilderness. That is when he fell.

Job had been attacked by Satan and captured mercilessly hundreds of years before. The full force of the curse that Satan wielded in the earth was hurled at him and his family:

> *And there was a day when his sons and his daughters were eating and drinking wine in their eldest brother's house: And there came a messenger unto Job, and said, The oxen were plowing, and the asses feeding beside them:* ***And the Sabeans fell upon them, and took them away; yea, they have slain the servants with the edge of the sword; and I only am escaped alone to tell thee.*** *While he was yet*

> *speaking, there came also another, and said,* ***The fire of God is fallen from heaven, and hath burned up the sheep, and the servants, and consumed them****; and I only am escaped alone to tell thee. While he was yet speaking, there came also another, and said,* ***The Chaldeans made out three bands, and fell upon the camels, and have carried them away, yea, and slain the servants with the edge of the sword****; and I only am escaped alone to tell thee. While he was yet speaking, there came also another, and said,* ***Thy sons and thy daughters were eating and drinking wine in their eldest brother's house: And, behold, there came a great wind from the wilderness, and smote the four corners of the house, and it fell upon the young men, and they are dead****; and I only am escaped alone to tell thee.*
>
> —Job 1:13–19 KJV, emphasis mine

All this was the power of Satan on full display. Job was powerless against it all. He had no authority or power to tread on serpents and scorpions. He was helpless. Jesus was not there to rescue him. God had no legal recourse to stop Satan's besiegement.

The interesting thing is that Jesus faced, in some way, all the same circumstances that Job faced, but with a very different result. He stood in the face of sickness and death, never flinching. He ruled, with absolute gravity, the forces of darkness. Everything Job endured would have been a short ordeal if Jesus had been there to cancel Satan's work in Job's life. The book of Job would have been very short if Jesus had been there! Can you imagine how the Scripture would have conveyed the story? It might have gone something like this:

> And there was a day when his sons and his daughters *were* eating and drinking wine in their eldest brother's house: And there came a messenger unto Job, and said, And the Sabeans fell upon them and have slain the servants with the edge of the sword; and I only am escaped alone to tell thee.
>
> As soon as Jesus heard the word that was spoken, he saith unto Job, Be not afraid, only believe. And he suffered no man to follow him, save Peter, and James, and John the brother of James. And he cometh to the house of Job, and seeth the tumult, and them that wept and wailed greatly. And when he was come in, he saith unto them, Why make ye this ado, and weep? they are not dead, but sleepeth. And they laughed him to scorn. But when he had put them all out, he taketh Job, and them that were with him, and entereth in where the servants were lying. And he said unto them, Arise! And straightway they

arose, and walked; And Job was astonished with a great astonishment.

Later on, there came also another, and said to Job, The fire of God is falling from heaven, and will burn up the sheep, and the servants to consume them; And, behold, there came a great wind from the wilderness, and is smiting the four corners of the house. Also thy sons and thy daughters *are* eating and drinking wine in their eldest brother's house.

And Jesus was asleep on a pillow: and Job awoke him, and said unto him, Master, carest thou not that we perish? And he arose, and rebuked the wind, and said unto the fire, Peace, be still. And the wind and fire ceased, and there was a great calm. And he said unto Job, Why are ye so fearful? how is it that ye have no faith? And Job feared exceedingly, and said, What manner of man is this, that even the wind and fire obey him?

While he *was* yet speaking, there came also another, and said, The Chaldeans made out three bands, and are attacking the camels, and will carry them away, yea, and will slay the servants with the edge of the sword. They are searching for you Master to carry you away as well. Jesus therefore, knowing all things, went forth, and said unto them, Whom seek

> ye? They answered him, Jesus of Nazareth. Jesus saith unto them, I am he. As soon then as he had said unto them, I am he, they went backward, and fell to the ground and he passing through the midst of them went his way and nothing was lost.

How very different Job's story would have been if only Jesus had been there! Job did not know Jesus, and therefore he experienced the power of the devil in his life. His sacrifices and fear-based prayers did nothing for him. If anything, it opened him up to the very suffering he was trying to avoid.

For three and a half years, Jesus, and by extension, His disciples, walked all over Satan and his demons—forgiving broken sinners, healing broken hearts and bodies, and casting devils out all over the place. At every turn, there was Jesus freeing men and women through simple faith. Satan had never encountered someone with such omnipotent force. Even the most righteous men had fallen before his authority in the past. No man was righteous, no, not one. I can imagine Satan deep in thought contemplating this "Jesus" and how all of this was possible. In his devious mind, he walked through a short history of men who had served God faithfully but whom he had defeated by temptation and sin on the one hand or by violence and murder on the other.

There was Abel and Noah and even Job. Yes, righteous Job. Not even Job went unscarred by my assault. But now

Jesus, another Son of God like the first, is here, and He is not even phased by the greatest of temptations. There is no sin in Him. He cannot be accused of even an impure motive.

When Jesus came on the scene, it was not a fair fight. Poor little devil.

Chapter 6

For Heaven's Sake!

"I will give you the keys of the kingdom of heaven; and whatever you bind on earth ***shall have been bound in heaven****, and whatever you loose on earth* ***shall have been loosed in heaven****."*

—Matthew 16:19 NASB, emphasis mine

Jesus not only had the weight of the world on His shoulders, but He carried the fate of heaven squarely on Himself as well. When Adam betrayed God and himself, it wasn't just man or the earth that felt the effects. Heaven and God Himself were now subject to the unwelcome treachery of Adam's sin! When God pronounced Adam's curse in Genesis 3, He was speaking of things beyond the earth. Heaven had been shaken, and the landscape of creation had been warped into a cursed shell of what God had created. There was a mixture in the heavenly court as well. To reference a movie, it was like a scene out of *The Lion King*, when Scar allowed the hyenas to invade and live in the pride land after Mufasa's death.

Matthew 16:19 reveals something interesting about heaven that might shock some Christians: Heaven, before Christ came, had some things that needed to be bound or imprisoned. Also, there were some things that were bound or restricted in heaven that had to be set free or loosed. Christ waged a war to take back the divine domain from its foreign invaders.

> *And* ***there was war in heaven****, Michael and his angels waging war with the dragon. The dragon and his angels waged war, and they (the dragon and his angels) were not strong enough,* ***and there was no longer a place found for them (the dragon and his angels) in heaven****.*
>
> —Revelation 12:7–8 NASB, emphasis mine

Satan and his angels had a place in heaven. Satan had moved in and had a permanent address in heaven. He used that place, which was a place of authority, to accuse Israel day and night.

> *Then I heard a loud voice in heaven, saying, "Now the salvation, and the power, and the kingdom of our God and the authority of His Christ have come,*

for the accuser of our brethren has been thrown down, he who accuses them before our God day and night."

—Revelation 12:10 NASB, emphasis mine

Satan had this place in heaven, and it is what gave him his authority in the earth. Truly this place was the place of Adam. Jesus came to save people! Jesus also came to save the earth. None of that was possible unless Jesus could save heaven first from these unwanted residents of the celestial realm.

Jesus prophesied boldly in John 12:31 (KJV):

Now is the judgment of this world: now shall the prince of this world be cast out.

Jesus was speaking of His soon coming death on the cross. The judgment of this world would start with its leader. Satan is the prince of this world, and he was cast out from his place of power. Satan was not cast out of the earth into hell. He was driven from God's presence above, down to the earth beneath. Jesus judged this world by permanently marooning its serpent king here until his doomed finale. The cross defanged the snake-prince by removing the sin that had so empowered him. The blood of Jesus fulfilled every requirement of the Law of God and redeemed man from the power of the devil.

This is the "Good" in the "Good News"! Jesus' salvation is so wonderful when we see what we have been rescued from completely.

The Turning Point

God is *good*! Jesus truly paid it all! Revelation 12:5–12 (NASB, emphasis mine) reveals a "behind the scenes" look at what exactly happened when Jesus completed the work of redeeming mankind:

> ***And she gave birth to a son, a male child, who is to rule all the nations with a rod of iron; and her child was caught up to God and to His throne****....* *And there was war in heaven, Michael and his angels waging war with the dragon. The dragon and his angels waged war, and they were not strong enough, and there was no longer a place found for them in heaven. And the great dragon was thrown down, the serpent of old who is called the devil and Satan, who deceives the whole world; he was thrown down to the earth, and his angels were thrown down with him. Then I heard a loud voice in heaven, saying, "****Now the salvation, and the power, and the kingdom of our God and the authority of His Christ have come, for the accuser of our brethren has been thrown down, he who accuses***

> ***them before our God day and night****. And they overcame him because of the blood of the Lamb and because of the word of their testimony, and they did not love their life even when faced with death.* ***For this reason, rejoice, O heavens and you who dwell in them.*** *Woe to the earth and the sea, because the devil has come down to you, having great wrath, knowing that he has only a short time."*

Even though this is a passage from the book of Revelation, it illustrates something that happened in the past when Jesus came to the earth and set us free. It is a condensed picture of the life of Jesus from His birth to His ascension into heaven. The words **"who is to rule all the nations with a rod of iron"** is a prophecy from Psalm 2:9 that speaks of the Messiah. In Revelation 2:27, Jesus has received authority from the Father, and He rules in the same prescribed phrasing written in Revelation 12:5:

> *And* ***he shall rule them with a rod of iron****; as the vessels of a potter shall they be broken to shivers:* ***even as I received of my Father****.*
>
> —Revelation 2:27 KJV, emphasis mine

Jesus is the One who was caught up to God and rules with a rod of iron. Verse 10 of Revelation 12 describes this as "salvation" and the "authority of His Christ." Then, in

Revelation 12:10 (NASB), the author reveals the reason salvation and Christ's authority have come:

> *"For the accuser of our brethren has been thrown down, he who accuses them before our God day and night."*

Salvation starts with Satan and his accusing angels being thrown out of heaven, no longer having a voice to speak their condemning allegations. When Jesus ascended into heaven, there was a war that had been fought in His name because of what He had done for us at the cross. His blood was the fuel that burned down the kingdom of darkness in heaven. There was a cleansing in heaven itself.

> *Moreover he* ***sprinkled with blood both the tabernacle****, and all the vessels of the ministry. And almost all things are by the law purged with blood; and without shedding of blood is no remission.* ***It was therefore necessary that the patterns of things in the heavens should be purified with these; but the heavenly things themselves with better sacrifices than these.***
>
> —Hebrews 9:21–23 KJV, emphasis mine

> *It was therefore necessary on the one hand that the representations of the things in the heavens [the*

> *earthly tent] should be* ***cleansed*** *constantly with these [animal sacrifices], but on the other hand,* ***the heavenly things*** *themselves* ***with better sacrifices than these [the blood of the Lord Jesus]. For*** *not into holy places constructed by human hands* ***did Messiah enter****, which are the types of the genuine [holy places], but* ***into heaven itself****.*
>
> —Hebrews 9:23–28 WUEST, emphasis mine

Jesus cleansed heaven with His own blood! Heaven had been invaded by a darkness that God was to wipe out through His Son! The Old Testament Tabernacle and all its furniture was cleansed by the blood of animals as a foreshadowing of the blood of Jesus being applied to heaven to "purge" it, as the King James Version puts so accurately. The Tabernacle, and later the Temple, were a type or model of heaven itself. The animal blood represented Jesus' own blood applied to heaven to remove the impurities that had rooted themselves into heaven's culture. The devil *had* a place in heaven until Jesus removed him by His own blood! Holy human blood destroyed the devil's power and cast him out of heaven forever.

Satan's power was accusation. The force of this power was the Law itself. Satan lost his ability to condemn man. Humans could resume their citizenship in heaven once again. Adam had sold his birthright for the forbidden bite, but Jesus won it back, as a man, for all mankind.

Job had felt the fanged injection flowing from that heavenly place secured by satanic strategy. He knew all too well that man did not possess a righteousness that could thwart the accusing onslaught from that heavenly seat of judgment. Job had lived a perfect life, and it meant nothing. It stopped nothing. Satan had full authority in Job's life because Satan's authority came from heaven. The meat of the book of Job is the discussion that ensues between Job and his three friends to explain why this trial was allowed to consume Job. What had he done to deserve such absolute desolation? What curse had he uttered to anger God and incur His wrath? In the book, Job spends his time defending his honor and uncovering the different proofs of his very just conduct. Back and forth, the book weaves a tapestry of dialogue between baseless accusations from Job's friends and futile apologetics from Job. Oddly enough, this is the very thing most people do when they encounter hard circumstances, either personally or when a close acquaintance suffers nearby in life. They ruminate, looking for the good or the bad, defending or accusing themselves or others of shortcomings. The truth was beyond Job's eyes or the eyes of his friends. They were not given insight into the workings of heaven. Like drunk men in the dark, blinded by an ignorance to their own blindness, they fumbled and stumbled for a righteous explanation. In other words, they did not know what they did not know. They had failed to see that the sin feeding this fire was not Job's imperfections, but Adam's transgression. A transgression so mighty in its effect, its waves crashed across heaven's boundaries, soaking the beautiful city with its stench. This is the sin Jesus purged from heaven. His blood was so pure and powerful that nothing could stand against its omnipotent, holy fury! Michael could finally execute the "Blood" order. I believe he had been waiting for this moment for millennia. Satan had paraded so brazenly through the courts of God's city, and Michael the archangel had to watch with frustration—a frustration building with no outlet. Then suddenly, without warning, there was a roar and a rush booming through the holy halls. Can you imagine the sounds and movements through those paved streets when Jesus set foot for the first time on that hallowed ground? Heaven began to shake, and there was a call to angelic arms! A new King had just arrived in heaven. A human King walked down the boulevard of glory for the first time since Adam's fall. Behind Him came an army never encountered before nor since. Michael and his angels, now empowered by the blood of the Lamb, began this final and eternal cleansing. It began with John the Baptist's birth and Jesus immaculate conception, followed by His birth. It would finish with the resurrected, ascended King of man taking His rightful place at the right hand of God, our Father.

Peace in Heaven

There was a shaking in heaven. In the first covenant, there was a shaking, and when Jesus activated this final new covenant, there was a shaking in the heavenly city. When the Law of Moses was given on Mount Sinai, God came down onto that mountain, and the earth quaked under the magnificent pressure of His presence. Violently did the earth shudder when God pressed His foot upon its soil. Israel saw the might of God as the earth heaved back and forth, and it was a fearful thing there at Sinai. As distressing and, at the same time, amazing as this encounter was with the Lord at the giving of the Law, it paled in its effect when compared to the shaking of Jesus' ascension into the heavenly Jerusalem. God shook heaven, and everything that was not supposed to be there came hurtling out of its gates, crashing to the earth.

> *See that ye refuse not him that speaketh. For if they escaped not who refused him that spake on earth, much more shall not we escape, if we turn away from him that speaketh from heaven: Whose voice then shook the earth: but now he hath promised, saying,* ***Yet once more I shake not the earth only, but also heaven.*** *And this word, Yet once more, signifieth the removing of those things that are*

> *shaken, as of things that are made, that those things which cannot be shaken may remain. Wherefore we receiving a kingdom which cannot be moved, let us have grace, whereby we may serve God acceptably with reverence and godly fear: For our God is a consuming fire.*
>
> —Hebrews 12:25–29 KJV, emphasis mine

The writer of Hebrews in these verses and the whole of chapter 12 is speaking in contrasting effect to compare the Old Testament and the New Testament. God shook heaven free of everything that did not possess His eternal nature. There was a divine spark referred to as eternal life that Jesus gave to us when we believe the Gospel. The devil had no spark. He was created, and he possessed nothing of God's nature. When Jesus, as a man, ascended from the earth and set His foot upon that golden highway, just like what occurred at Sinai, there was a holy trembling throughout heaven's land. His glory pierced through every molecule and element in the blessed metropolis. Everything reacted and shook with joy to God and revenge at the imposing trespassers. The all-consuming fire of God was felt in that place. I cannot prove it, but I believe heaven's gold was not clear before Jesus achieved His ransacking of hell and death. Revelation says all the gold of the street of heaven is as clear as glass. There is no doubt in my mind that the glory unleashed through Jesus by God washed everything in holy fire, provoking such purity in even the precious metals that overlaid the streets. Truth itself was infused into the atomic workings of all persons and materials alike. Plants and animals both were glorified. Angels were brighter and sang with exuberance. God's glory exploded across heaven and...it *shook*. Everything shook, and Satan, with his accusations and his schemes, was shaken out of God's presence, no longer given permission or access to the blessed city.

On the precipice of Jesus' plunge toward the cross and death, He entered Jerusalem riding on a donkey. The multitude of disciples gathered to welcome Him in His royal procession, and they gave praise to God. There was a prophetic declaration spoken by His disciples that contained a very peculiar phrase:

> *And when he was come nigh, even now at the descent of the mount of Olives, the whole multitude of the disciples began to rejoice and praise God with a loud voice for all the mighty works that they had seen; saying,* **Blessed *be* the King that cometh in the name of the Lord: *peace in heaven***, *and glory in the highest.*
>
> —Luke 19:37–38 KJV, emphasis mine

"Peace in heaven"! There was a revelation in that song of the effect of the coming of the King in the name of the Lord. His coming would bring peace in heaven. Up to this point, there had been constant conflict, but now heaven was on the brink of peace. When Jesus shook heaven, everything that was adversarial left. The troublemaker was exorcised, and there was a restoration of heaven. His name is the Prince of Peace, and He brought an end to the conflict of Adam before God. Accusation, contention, and opposition were no more.

Paul saw something in the mystery of the Gospel concerning heaven and Christ's blood. He wrote about it to the Colossians:

> *And, having made peace through the blood of his cross, by him to reconcile all things unto himself; by him, I say, whether they be things in earth, or things in heaven.*
>
> —Colossians 1:20 KJV

Peace, according to this verse, involves reconciliation. Jesus made peace in heaven through His holy blood. How did He accomplish this feat? His blood was able to reconcile the irreconcilable. Satan had a legal place in heaven to stand against humanity and accuse man before God. He had a position of contention and aggravation over anything concerning the earth. Adam had lost all, but Jesus returned to us everything by His blood. Heaven was quiet once more. Satan's noise had been silenced. In his place stood the Prince of Peace. Jesus had delivered heaven from the enemy's grasp, and there was seen "glory in the highest" once more!

Heaven celebrated with exuberance over the victorious banishment of the enemy of humanity!

Paul gives us a picture of the scene in heaven when Jesus defeated Satan and the other accusing demons. Paul quoted from Psalm 68 when he wrote Ephesians 4:8 to describe Jesus' triumphant march through heaven:

> *Wherefore he saith, When he ascended up on high, he led captivity captive, and gave gifts unto men.*
>
> —Ephesians 4:8 KJV

The *God's Word* translation brings out some of the meaning of this verse more clearly:

That's why the Scriptures say:

> *"When he went to the highest place,*
> *he took captive those who had captured us*
> *and gave gifts to people."*

Paul says that when Jesus went into heaven, he took captivity captive. He imprisoned the very thing that had been imprisoning humanity. Satan and his minions were led in a procession of defeat right down the middle of heaven's streets. This verse gives the picture of a victorious king after the battle has been won who is coming back into the city and celebrating with a glorious parade. The defeated foes would follow behind the champion king, defeated and in shame. This is what happened when Jesus went to the highest place, captured our enemies, and paraded them before all of heaven. This did not happen as Jesus was going up to heaven. This happened after He arrived in heaven. The defeat of Satan and his group took place in heaven. They were captured in heaven. They were paraded in heaven, and then they were cast out (John 12:31). One commentary has translated the text to help show the order of these events: "Having ascended into (the) heights he led captive captivity."[1]

This captivity was the same captivity mentioned in Job 42:9–10 (KJV, emphasis mine):

> *And the LORD turned* ***the captivity of Job****, when he prayed for his friends.*

Jesus captured the same captivity that captured Job. It has now been defeated and dethroned. Colossians 2:15

---

1 Graham, G. (2008) *An Exegetical Summary of Ephesians*. 2nd ed. Dallas, TX: SIL International, p. 293.

sums up precisely what Jesus did to the enemy before all the occupants of heaven:

> *He stripped all the spiritual tyrants in the universe of their sham authority at the Cross and* ***marched them naked through the streets****.*
>
> —Colossians 2:15 MSG, emphasis mine

> *And on that cross Christ freed himself from the power of the spiritual rulers and authorities;* ***he made a public spectacle of them by leading them as captives in his victory procession****.*
>
> —Colossians 2:15 GNB, emphasis mine

This was absolute defeat on display without reservation. No mercy was given to the enemy of mankind. Jesus made it clear this was total desolation of the enemies of God, and He did this in your name. He did it for you!

There was a gushing joy that was unleashed as righteousness swept through the celestial city. As Satan was flung from his heavenly habitation, laughter flowed freely from the throne of God down the gleaming boulevard of Heaven.

After Satan was cast out, a proclamation was made **"For this reason, rejoice, O heavens and you who dwell in them."**

God was laughing—laughing with joy at the sweeping victory His Son had secured. Jesus had done it. The plan of God had worked.

He that sitteth in the heavens shall laugh.

—Psalm 2:4 KJV

And laugh He did!

Chapter 7

Reigning as Kings

All the previously stated teaching leads to an amazing set of truths that collaborate with the supreme power of God called the Gospel. The Gospel is the "Good News," or the "prosperous message" of what God has done for you and me through Jesus to set us free from the same tyranny that had robbed everything from Job. We are set free! Jesus came into this world and became human that He might save humanity and create a new race of men, men who rule over devils and are not ruled by them. He shed His pure blood and redeemed us from the enemy's power. He raised us out of hell and seated us in heavenly places to reign as kings. He cleansed heaven and prepared a place for us to dwell with Him. All this was possible because He removed the sin that was separating us from God and binding humanity to an alliance with Satan. Ultimately, He had to cleanse heaven so He could cleanse us and our hearts. He removed that accusing voice of judgment from the courts of heaven so He could release us from the prosecuting voices living in our hearts. Redemption ignites the artistry in every man's heart:

> Death dethroned by the Man,
> Man now living in God's plan
>
> Sin and Death have lost their Realm
> God's Man now at the Helm
>
> Now Man's soul, white as snow
> Jesus rose and made him whole
>
> Death's devils are defeated
> In Christ, Man succeeded!

The eighth chapter of Romans is to the Christian what the Bill of Rights is to American citizens. The entire chapter is a treatise on the rights secured for us by our Lord. Everything He did for us and what we have as a result is set forth in concise statements throughout this treasure-dense chapter! After going through all Jesus has done for us, Paul ends the chapter with some conclusions about where we now stand before God. Romans 8:33–34 declares freedom for mankind from the very same power that took Job down.

> *Who shall lay any thing to the charge of God's elect?* It is *God that justifieth. Who* is *he that condemneth?* It is *Christ that died, yea rather, that*

is risen again, who is even at the right hand of God, who also maketh intercession for us.

—Romans 8:33–34 KJV

And who would dare tangle with God by messing with one of God's chosen? Who would dare even to point a finger?

—Romans 8:33–34 MSG

Who can bring an accusation against God's elect? God is the One who justifies. Who is the one who condemns? Christ Jesus is the One who died, but even more, has been raised; He also is at the right hand of God and intercedes for us.

—Romans 8:33–34 HCSB

Satan has been removed, and there is nobody now accusing you before God. "Who would dare even to point a finger?"

What then shall we say to this? If God is on our side, who is there to appear against us?

—Romans 8:31, *The New Testament in Modern Speech*

There is no one up in heaven anymore to even appear against you to accuse you before God. Satan has vacated the premises.

> *There is* ***therefore now no condemnation*** *to them which are in Christ Jesus, who walk not after the flesh, but after the Spirit.*
>
> —Romans 8:1 KJV, emphasis mine

There is only one voice in heaven now speaking for you and about you to God. That is not the voice of shame and condemnation, but of justification. Jesus speaks of you in prayer to God in the same way He speaks to God about Himself. That is the voice that represents you in God's presence. In the Old Testament, the voice that spoke for man was satanic. It accused day and night. Its purpose was to condemn humanity for its sin. In the New Testament, Jesus speaks the words of His blood. They are super-powered words, when spoken to God, that cause man to stand in a place of complete favor with God eternally. These words were purchased with the blood of Jesus.

> *But ye are come unto mount Sion, and unto the city of the living God, the heavenly Jerusalem, and to an innumerable company of angels, to the general assembly and church of the firstborn, which are written in heaven, and to God the Judge of all, and*

> *to the spirits of just men made perfect, and to Jesus the mediator of the new covenant, and to the blood of sprinkling, that* ***speaketh*** *better things than that of Abel.*
>
> —Hebrews 12:22–24 KJV, emphasis mine

Scripturally, when blood is shed, there is a message spoken from the victim's blood that only God can hear. Really, it is the cry of the soul that has been released through death from the physical body. The soul of man has a cry unto God for holy vengeance when they have been killed unjustly. In Revelation 6:9–10 (KJV), we are allowed to listen in to the outcries of the righteous calling for justice on their murderers:

> *And when he had opened the fifth seal, I saw under the altar the souls of them that were slain for the word of God, and for the testimony which they held: And they cried with a loud voice, saying, How long, O Lord, holy and true, dost thou not judge and avenge our blood on them that dwell on the earth?*

We first see this phenomenon in the death of Abel. Cain kills Abel out of jealousy. God confronts Cain about the crime with these words:

> *And he said, What hast thou done? the voice of thy brother's blood crieth unto me from the ground.*
>
> —Genesis 4:10 KJV

Abel's blood was crying from the ground about what Cain had done. It was an accusing voice before God about Cain, which incited God's judgment on him. Hebrews 12:24 (KJV) contrasts Jesus and Abel, saying, "the blood of sprinkling, that speaketh better things than *that of* Abel." Jesus' blood has a greater message than that of revenge or accusation. Jesus gathered His shed blood and sprinkled it all over heaven, and when it touched the ground, there was a cry that went up to God's holy throne. Whatever that cry was from His blood, God was going to react in holy execution. Jesus could have accused us of His death. He could have demanded retribution on humanity. He could have interceded for Himself, but He did not. Jesus' blood spoke out, and its message was, *"grace"*! That is what God heard in heaven, and He is still hearing it today.

When Job's name was brought up to God in heaven, there was no grace or righteousness, but an abundance of accusations. Job served God perfectly, but the voice that represented Job in heaven was still full of accusation. That is all God heard concerning Job. Now when your name is brought up to God, Jesus is the One talking, and all He has to say about you is righteous and perfect. That is all God hears from our Advocate. There is no dissenting voice against you in the throne room. Jesus is constantly talking about how blessed and righteous you are because of His grace-saturated blood!

> *Seeing then that* **we have a great high priest**, *that is passed into the heavens, Jesus the Son of God, let us hold fast our profession.... Let us therefore* **come boldly** *unto the throne of grace, that we may obtain mercy, and find grace to help in time of need.*
>
> —Hebrews 4:14, 16 KJV, emphasis mine

We are now called to come boldly before God to obtain grace and mercy. That means that even when we sin or mess up, we are to be bold in God's throne room in our obtaining of mercy and grace. God does not accept shame and condemnation as penance for sin. Jesus has paid it all for us, and He now represents us. We are to be bold "that we may obtain mercy." In other words, if we are to obtain mercy, it must be with boldness before God. That is all He respects or accepts. He is not moved by your self-flagellations. He is moved by a bold faith in the blood of Jesus, especially when you are aware of your need because of some transgression in time. God is not impressed when you beat yourself up out of a sense of guilt from which He paid to free you through Christ. Yes, we should experience a sorrow that leads to repentance, but that repentance must lead to faith in Christ or it can be as destructive as not repenting at all. I must turn away from my fleshly attempts to make amends with God, and boldly believe in the blood that speaks better things about me!

Some people still see a great cosmic court proceeding in heaven over their life. Many a sermon has been preached with dramatic narrative that describes a scene where Satan is standing before God accusing still, but then Jesus stands up at some point as our great legal Defender to make His case. The sermon continues with something along the lines of this: "Then Jesus says, 'But wait, behold the scars in My hands and My feet. Look at the hollowed scar in My side! My blood has forgiven them and saved them.' and then God declares us not guilty, leaving the devil in defeat once again...*until next time*."

The problem with this picture is that it is part of the Old Covenant. Before Christ came and redeemed us, as men found favor with God through the Mosaic Covenant, there were angels that interceded for them and against the adversary. Satan would accuse, and if you were a Jew, angels would react on your behalf to defend you based the covenant of the Law given through Moses. That was why it was so important to abide by every precept in the Law of Moses. Israel's obedience empowered the angels to protect and defend the people of God. If a man, or the nation, violated God's precepts, man fell under the dominion of death once again. We see this cycle repeated over and over throughout the Old Testament. Israel's keeping of the Law secures the nation against evil and judgment. God, through the angels, can act on their behalf through the Mosaic Covenant, but if there is sin, specifically a violation against those laws, then Israel faced death. The wages of sin is death! Death is not just the final departure from this earthly life. Death is biblically titled as the power that the devil wields. In other words, Satan's power is called death. If Satan is exerting any energy against someone, that energy is called death. In physics, power is sometimes referred to as activity. Activity is energy converted in time. When the devil is active, when he is burning calories, the energy that fuels that activity is called death. The devil's power is called death in Hebrews 2:14 (KJV, emphasis mine):

> *Forasmuch then as the children are partakers of flesh and blood, he also himself likewise took part of the same; that through death he might destroy him that had* ***the power of death, that is, the devil****.*

That power, under the Old Covenant, had sway when they violated the Law of God and did not seek atonement or covering for forgiveness for the transgression. Satan would have legal claim over the individual or nation. When Adam and Eve ate from the tree, God told them they would die.

God was not just foretelling the event of their physical death, but of a power that would rule every part of their lives.

There was a court proceeding recorded in the Old Testament from the prophet Zechariah:

> *And he shewed me Joshua the high priest standing before the angel of the LORD, and* ***Satan standing at his right hand to resist him****. And the LORD said unto Satan, The LORD rebuke thee, O Satan; Even the LORD that hath chosen Jerusalem rebuke thee: Is not this a brand plucked out of the fire?* ***Now Joshua was clothed with filthy garments, and stood before the angel.*** *And he answered and spake unto those that stood before him, saying, Take away the filthy garments from him. And unto him he said, Behold, I have caused thine iniquity to pass from thee, and I will clothe thee with change of raiment. And I said, Let them set a fair mitre upon his head. So they set a fair mitre upon his head, and clothed him with garments. And the angel of the LORD stood by.*
>
> —Zechariah 3:1–5 KJV, emphasis mine

Joshua, the high priest, was being opposed by Satan before God. Satan was resisting him. Why? Joshua was clothed with filthy garments in God's presence. The garments represented some iniquity in Joshua's life. He had committed some sin, and it empowered Satan against him. You will notice they stood before the angel of the Lord in these proceedings. God operated through the angels in the Old Testament. They acted as a type of "go-between" for God and man. They also acted as the defenders of God's people. There was an opposition (Satan) in heaven, as I have written before, but that is what Jesus removed. He eliminated that opposer called Satan. The angels and the blood of bulls and goats could never take away our sins before God. Only Jesus and His blood had that power. Nothing can stand in even basic accusation against that blood. The most the blood of a lamb could secure was a temporary covering that involved the powerful, but limited services of angels. When Jesus came, He brought us into another kingdom. He did not offer a covering for our sins. He washed them away completely. This was a permanent removal. An eternal washing away, as if it had never existed, as if it never was. He did not just take away our sins forever, but He gave us the gift of His own righteousness. To accuse you is to accuse Jesus. You have and are of the same righteousness as Christ Himself, because it is Christ Himself who has become our righteousness.

> *For he hath made him to be sin for us, who knew no sin; that* ***we might be made the righteousness of God in him****.*
>
> —2 Corinthians 5:21 KJV, emphasis mine

> *But of him are ye in* ***Christ Jesus****, who of God* ***is made unto us*** *wisdom, and* ***righteousness****, and sanctification, and redemption.*
>
> —1 Corinthians 1:30 KJV, emphasis mine

Christ is *our* Righteousness! The Lord Himself is *our* Righteousness!

> *Behold, the days come, saith the LORD, that* ***I will raise unto David a righteous Branch, and a King shall reign and prosper****, and shall execute judgment and justice in the earth.* ***In his days*** *Judah shall be saved, and Israel shall dwell safely: and* ***this is his name whereby he shall be called, THE LORD OUR RIGHTEOUSNESS****.*
>
> —Jeremiah 23:5–6 KJV, emphasis mine

Jeremiah here is prophesying that the name of the King, the Messiah, whom God will send to earth will be called "The Lord our Righteousness." He has become my righteousness so that I might become His righteousness. What a glorious gift! It is impenetrable to guilt, condemnation, and shame. There is no weakness or hidden loophole to it. God, under His omniscient, unbending, holy gaze, has tried this righteousness in eternal fires, and there are no defects or blemishes. It is the righteousness of God, and you stand empowered in it before God's holy presence!

You have received heaven's diplomatic immunity! There is no crime you can be charged with before God. No one is even allowed to talk to God about you except for Jesus. He represents you to God! Before Jesus, God was simply the Judge of these proceedings, and Satan had the legal right to rule humanity because of sin. Job was the perfect case study of just how far-reaching Satan's power was through Adam! God could only enforce the terms of this twisted alliance between Satan and man. God could not intervene on Job's behalf. He spoke to Satan about Job's righteousness, but it had no effect on the outcome. Fast-forward to what Christ has accomplished and how things have changed. Paul states a radical conclusion in Romans 8:

> *Moreover whom he did predestinate, them he also called: and whom he called, them* ***he also justified****: and* ***whom he justified, them he also glorified****.*

> *What shall we then say to these things?* ***If God be for us, who can be against us?***
>
> —Romans 8:30–31 KJV, emphasis mine

Due to this justification, God is now for us! If God, the Judge, has now taken our side and is now not against us or even a neutral party, but the unlimited defending force of unstoppable power and holiness, it is a logical question to ask: Who can be against us now? The question is rhetorical. The answer is so blatantly obvious: No one can be against you. Everything is on your side. Nothing is allowed to oppose you anymore.

The famous verses of Psalm 23 are fulfilled in Christ:

> ***Thou preparest a table before me in the presence of mine enemies:*** *Thou anointest my head with oil; my cup runneth over.*
>
> —Psalm 23:5 KJV, emphasis mine

The picture is of a man surrounded by enemies. The situation looks bleak. Survival would be a miracle. This is the valley of death about which David sang so poetically. Right in the middle of this valley, with adversaries having formed a perimeter around you, God is causing you not just to survive, but to feast in the face of your foes. The opposition disappears, and they become docile, observing bystanders of God's goodness in your life!

> *Surely goodness and mercy shall follow me all the days of my life: And I will dwell in the house of the Lord for ever.*
>
> —Psalm 23:6 KJV

The only thing seeking you now is goodness and mercy! You have no enemies in Christ. No one can hurt you anymore. You are hidden in Christ Jesus!

All things are now working together for your good! Creation is now on your side. Like Adam before the fall, and now Jesus, creation was created to serve its masters. God created everything for mankind to rule over as kings in the earth. Righteousness causes humanity to reign again. His righteousness places us in the middle of royalty. You now wear His signet ring of authority, and all creation, in Jesus' name, has to obey you.

> *For if by the transgression of the one, death reigned through the one, much more* ***those who receive*** *the abundance of grace and of* ***the gift of righteousness will reign (as kings) in life*** *through the One, Jesus Christ.*
>
> —Romans 5:17 NASB, emphasis mine

Through Jesus and the gift of righteousness, you are now a ruler in the earth. Job did not have access to this righteousness when he was captured. Satan was the ruler, and he used creation to execute evil against men like Job. Now we are called to reign supreme under Jesus. He is the King of kings. We are those kings whom He is ruling. We are called and created to reign in life. It did not say that we are going to reign in the life to come. Although that is true, that is not what is being referenced here. We are empowered with all the ingredients to reign *now*. Righteousness is the heart of this power, and faith is the heartbeat of our reign. We are believers because we are righteous. The righteous live by faith, and, I would add, we rule by faith also. Faith in the Bible is the behavior of kings. When a person in a Bible narrative believes, that person always stands in a position of authority with God. Jesus said it like this:

> *And the Lord said, "If you had faith like a mustard seed, you would say to this mulberry tree, 'Be uprooted and be planted in the sea'; and it would obey you."*
>
> —Luke 17:6 NASB

This verse stands out as one of the most amazing things Jesus ever said about faith, and in general. If you have faith… creation would obey you!!

It…would…obey…*you?*

What does that even mean? A tree, which has no perceived conscience, would respond directly to your faith? That is what Jesus said. He did not say the tree would respond to God. He did not say that God would respond to you. Jesus said that faith would cause the tree, or really anything in creation, to respond directly to you. In another passage, He said a mountain would do the same thing.

Also, Jesus indicated something just as odd about how faith would affect your actions or the way you perceived creation:

> *"If you had faith like a mustard seed, you would say to this…tree…"*

If you have faith, Jesus said you would start talking to trees? He did not say that you would talk to God about the tree or that God would talk to the tree, but that you would start talking directly to a tree or a mountain, telling it what to do. These are some of the most interesting verses in the Bible about the effects of faith and how it changes the way we interact with the world around us. Faith empowers you to be the king whom God created you to be. You will start talking to things and expecting results from your commands. Jesus promised that creation would respond to you just like it responded to Him when He was on the earth. Job did not start telling the wind to stop…or commanding angels to fight his battles…or binding the devil that was binding him. One simple reason: Job was a servant, not a king.

> *And Jehovah saith unto the Adversary, "Hast thou set thy heart against* ***My servant*** *Job?'*
>
> —Job 1:8 YLT, emphasis mine

We are called "sons of God" now. We are no longer servants or slaves. You are a king in God's court!

> *Therefore you are no longer a slave but a son, and if a son, then an heir of God through Christ.*
>
> —Galatians 4:7 NKJV

Jesus spoke to the wind and the waves, to devils and demons, to trees and fish. He spoke as a King. He spoke as a man was supposed to speak. He is our example!

> *And we know that* ***all things work together for good*** *to them that love God, to them who are the called according to his purpose.* ***For*** *whom he did foreknow, he also did predestinate to be* ***conformed to the image of his Son****, that he might be the firstborn among many brethren. Moreover whom he did predestinate, them he also called: and whom he called, them he also justified: and whom he justified, them he also glorified.*
>
> —Romans 8:28–30 KJV, emphasis mine

These verses are the ultimate descriptor of what we truly have at our disposal because of what God has done for us. These verses have also been used by countless Christians and preachers alike to promote a false picture of what God is up to in the universe. These verses were supposed to empower you in Christ, and yet most Christians have been made willing, passive victims of the enemy by a misunderstanding of Romans 8:28. This verse is generally tied to the same misgivings as the book of Job: "All these bad things happened to Job, but God caused all the bad things to really work out for Job's best interest." What a crass, obtuse treatment of the Word of God. Preachers with little to no understanding of the redemption they claim to spread have facilitated such preposterous ideas.

"All things" mean *all things*. Creation is the "all things" that is being spoken about here. The universe is the "all things" that is now starting to work for our good instead of the hijacked version that was constantly against us.

When Adam sinned, God gave him an accurate description of what life on earth was going to be like as a result of his sin:

> *And unto Adam he said, Because thou hast hearkened unto the voice of thy wife, and hast eaten of the tree, of which I commanded thee, saying, Thou shalt not eat of it:* ***cursed is the ground for***

> ***thy sake;*** *in* ***sorrow shalt thou eat of it*** *all the days of thy life;* ***thorns also and thistles shall it bring forth to thee****; and thou shalt eat the herb of the field;* ***in the sweat of thy face shalt thou eat bread****, till thou return unto the ground; for out of it wast thou taken:* ***for dust thou art****, and unto dust shalt thou return.*
>
> —Genesis 3:17–19 KJV, emphasis mine

This earth was designed by God to produce Eden. It was created to grow paradise for mankind, but Adam sinned, and it started producing thorns, thistles, sorrows, and sweat until we become the very dust that fights against us until we die. But now we are kings, and all of creation is for us. The trees obey us, and the mountains move at our command. Even the air is on our side.

Why is this happening? Why has creation done a complete 180-degree turnaround?

Because you have been "conformed to the image of his Son, that he might be the firstborn among many brethren" (Romans 8:29 KJV)!

Jesus is the firstborn, and we are now His brothers, made to have the exact same nature as Jesus. We have the same Father, and we have been conformed to the image of God's own Son. We are not stepchildren of God. We are not secondary sons, but in Christ, we are equal to Christ in His relationship to the Father.

We are heirs of God and joint heirs with Christ. Everything He has is mine, and everything He is, God has conformed me to be.

We now reign with Christ. We reign with unlimited power and influence. We reign in the place of death itself.

> *For if by one man's offence* ***death reigned by one****; much more* ***they*** *which receive abundance of grace and of the gift of righteousness* ***shall reign in life by one****, Jesus Christ.*
>
> —Romans 5:17 KJV, emphasis mine

Death took the throne of man away from man through one man's sin. Jesus, as a Man, took back that throne by dying for the one man's offense who gave up the throne, and now through Christ, we have the right to sit on that throne again in Him! We now sit in the same seat of influence as Death itself sat. That is amazing power in Jesus' name. You are now able to reign in life the same way Death reigned in your life before Christ.

You are now seated in heavenly places in Christ!

Chapter 8

Silencing the Little Satan Inside

Which shew the work of the law written in their hearts, their conscience also bearing witness, and their thoughts the mean while accusing or else excusing one another.

—Romans 2:15 KJV

And having an high priest over the house of God; let us draw near with a true heart in full assurance of faith, having our hearts sprinkled from an evil conscience, and our bodies washed with pure water.

—Hebrews 10:20–21 KJV

Awareness was the very first result of the sin of Adam and Eve. They became aware of themselves. They became aware of their own nakedness. This naked vulnerability gave way quickly to fear, and then self-preservation. Sin was taking over in rapid fashion, and it would not be long before the accusations came pouring out. Adam blamed God and Eve. Eve said the "devil made me do it." It was not in those exact words, but the idea was the same. Interestingly, Satan never defends himself. I believe God created us with a conscience, but it was not intended to be an alarm system of right and wrong. The conscience is tied to the heart of man. It was to be a device to fill man with an awareness or knowledge. That is what the "conscience" means: "with knowledge." There are two competing sets of knowledge in the Bible: self-generated knowledge and the knowledge of God. The first is attained from our own experiences apart from anything God generates. The other knowledge comes by God's Spirit, and we are completely dependent on God to reveal this information to us. One knowledge leads us away from God and will result in death eventually. The other knowledge is from God and allows mankind to partake of God's own life and nature.

In the garden of Eden, Adam and Eve had a choice of how they wanted to do life. They could know good and evil for themselves or through a relationship with God. They chose to rely on themselves and rejected God and His warning. Death has been the result ever since. Jesus, we know, came to redeem us back from all this death and destruction. Through His blood, He has cleansed us from our sins before

God and even cleansed heaven itself. There is only one thing that stands between you and experiencing the fullness of all Jesus has done for you: *you*. Sin, death, and Satan have been eliminated. You are the last enemy of your own soul. That inward accusing voice that reminds and reviews your past. Whether it is twenty years, two weeks, or two minutes ago, the relentless voice of conscience can be the most oppressive voice in your life. Your conscience must come under the washing of the blood of Jesus. What does that mean? Isn't that what happens when I repent and ask for forgiveness? It should be, but for many, they believe they are forgiven by God but continue to flog themselves under the scrutiny called self-condemnation. There is an internal Satan in all of us that must be flushed out. I do not mean to say that if you have done something wrong and your conscience reacts in abhorrence, it should ignored. In fact, the Holy Spirit can use that, and He does use that to bring repentance. But when I have repented, there must be a complete cleansing. Our reliance on the blood of Jesus must be so thorough that we cannot allow any rummaging around in the past to be tolerated. There can only be a complete severing of the awareness of what we did wrong from our minds if we are going to experience the full cleansing power of the blood of Jesus upon our consciences.

Adam and Eve invited Satan into their conscience. The conscience became a tool of the devil to keep mankind aware of his sins. That awareness drowned man in guilt and drowned God out of his landscape. He knew God was there, but he had no awareness of his reality. Faint shadows and fading memories are what mankind is left with now. Then Jesus comes, and He opens our eyes again to God. It is not that we just know of God, but we become aware of Him presently. His righteousness touches everything again, and we are made alive with His life.

> *And having an high priest over the house of God; let us draw near with a true heart in full assurance of faith, having our hearts sprinkled from an evil conscience, and our bodies washed with pure water.*
>
> —Hebrews 10:21–22 KJV

The heart is sprinkled with the blood of Jesus from a conscience of evil. This means that your awareness of all the evil you have done is replaced with an intuition for God's grace. You become sensitive to God instead of sin. God wanted us to be filled with Him, but Adam chose this knowledge of good and evil. The blood sets you free from it all.

Job spent all that time looking at himself, with his friends examining him, looking for the imperfections and findings of what had brought such severe destruction on Job. They never realized their examinations of Job were the real issue. They were filled, not with God, but with themselves apart from God. Interestingly, when did Job become free from his captivity? Chapter after chapter left him reeling with pain and confusion, but when God revealed Himself and Job's eyes were opened to God for the first time in his life, he forgot about himself. He did not want to talk anymore. Read Job's own words:

> *Then Job answered the LORD, and said, I know that thou canst do every thing, and that no thought can be withholden from thee. Who is he that hideth counsel without knowledge? therefore have I uttered that I understood not; things too wonderful for me,* **which I knew not**. *Hear, I beseech thee, and I will speak: I will demand of thee, and declare thou unto me.* ***I have heard of thee by the hearing of the ear: But now mine eye seeth thee.*** *Wherefore I abhor myself, and repent In dust and ashes.*
>
> —Job 42:1–6 KJV, emphasis mine

He was set free from himself. He saw God, and that brought repentance. Job was not repenting of some broken commandment, but from living out of his own self-generated knowledge. He realized he did not actually know God for himself until that day when they met. His eyes were opened, and something changed in Job forever. He really saw Jesus that day, and he was set free.

The next part of Job's story is my personal favorite. Job has now seen God. God is angry with Job's three friends because of the way they had judged Job and accused him. They had let Satan use them to beat Job down even further.

> *And it was so, that after the LORD had spoken these words unto Job, the LORD said to Eliphaz the Temanite, My wrath is kindled against thee, and against thy two friends: for ye have not spoken of me the thing that is right, as my servant Job hath.* ***Therefore take unto you now seven bullocks and seven rams, and go to my servant Job, and offer up for yourselves a burnt offering; and my servant Job shall pray for you: for him will I accept:*** *lest I deal with you after your folly, in that ye have not spoken of me the thing which is right, like my servant Job. So Eliphaz the Temanite and Bildad the Shuhite and Zophar the Naamathite went, and did according as the LORD commanded them:* ***the LORD also accepted Job. And the LORD turned the captivity of Job, when he prayed for his friends: also the LORD gave Job twice as much as he had before.***
>
> —Job 42:7–10 KJV, emphasis mine

Remember how this whole thing started? We saw Job sacrificing for his children. He was afraid, and he was offering burnt offerings for each of his children based on the fear that they might have inadvertently cursed God. The fear was that sudden judgment might come on them because of some sin in their life. Job was diligent, but in the end, it did not help in the slightest. His kids died anyway, and he lost everything. This is the opening scene to Job's story.

Now we fast-forward to the end of the book of Job, and we see Job is to offer sacrifices for his friends to be forgiven by God and not incur His judgment for their self-righteousness. Look at what happens: God accepts Job! Job is not acting out of a sinful conscience, but out of a revelation of God. God has commanded the sacrifices, and this time they work.

Then something peculiar happens—Job prays for his friends, and when he prays, he is set free from his own captivity. Job first has his eyes on God instead of himself. Then, while still hurting from his loss and the pain of his illness, he begins to act in love and minister to others. His eyes are not on himself, but on God and the needs of others. That is what sets him free.

Jesus has come to set you free from the "little Satan" within who stands accusing day and night. This voice feeds off the knowledge of good and evil. The more you are filled with the awareness of yourself, the less you will have of the knowledge of God. Life cannot be about you. It has to be about God and the love He gives us for others. When you sit down to pray or when you stand to praise, the inner voice will rise to strip you in shame before God. Every bad thing you have done suddenly finds new life, invading your heart, and you find yourself naked and afraid, hiding behind your religious fig leaves. That is not God accusing you. It is not even the devil. That voice is you, filled with the knowledge of your shortcomings. Read the verses below and consider them in light of all we have been writing about:

> *This is how we know what love is: Jesus Christ laid down his life for us. And we ought to lay down our lives for our brothers and sisters. If anyone has material possessions and sees a brother or sister in need but has no pity on them, how can the love of God be in that person? Dear children, let us not love with words or speech but with actions and in truth.* ***This is how we know that we belong to the truth and how we set our hearts at rest in his presence:*** *If our hearts condemn us, we know that* ***God is greater than our hearts****, and he knows everything. Dear friends, if our hearts do not condemn us, we have confidence before God and receive from him anything we ask, because we keep his commands and do what pleases him.* ***And this is his command: to believe in the name of his Son, Jesus Christ, and to love one another***

> ***as he commanded us.*** *The one who keeps God's commands lives in him, and he in them. And this is how we know that he lives in us: We know it by the Spirit he gave us.*
>
> —1 John 3:16–24 NIV, emphasis mine

It sounds like John is prescribing the same thing that set Job free from his captivity.

Believe on the name of Jesus (instead of focusing on yourself and relying on your good works), and love one another (just like Job did by forgetting about his problems and even his failures and praying for his friends). Loving others calms our hearts in His presence. We shut down the accusations of the self-absorbed conscience by being submerged in *His* lovc for others!

> *Herein is our love made perfect, that we may have boldness in the day of judgment: because as he is, so are we in this world.*
>
> —1 John 4:17 KJV

Love fuses us with a confidence that silences every lying voice and every accusing voice in our world. The end of Job's story is a consummation of the silencing of so many voices in Job's life. Satan was finally silenced. Job's friends were silenced. In the end, Job himself was silenced. There were so many opinions and judgments throughout Job's script, but none spoke accurately. All these voices were the incessant collective buzz, like a plague of flesh flies, swarming Job in a darkness that drowns out all truth and light. God revealed Himself in a tornado that swept away all the detractors and distractions so that Job was left with only one voice to capture his attention. He was opened and exposed to God's light, and it drove out all the gray thoughts that had leeched themselves into Job's mind. Job the servant was replaced by the Job the king. Job emerged bold and free. Love does that to a man. God's love frees us from our own self-doubts and timidity. Cowardice is reduced to mere vapors before Jesus, and in its place, He erects a bold new man, lifted by God's words. Job realized he knew nothing of what he was speaking in such sure tones just minutes before, but now there was silence. Nothing. Job put his hand over his own mouth and repented. He was not repenting of sin in its traditional sense. He was turning from all he thought he knew about God. Baptized in the light-beams of seeing God in substance and truth, he was altered forever. Job would never be the same. Job starts out in a fearful state of superstitious sacrificing, ineffective on all accounts; he winds his way through a dialogue of confusion, despair, self-defense, and allegations to find himself face-to-face with the God he believes he knows so well. It is here, when he sees Him, that he suddenly sees himself first in abhorrence, but ultimately as God intended, like God

Himself. Job was silenced at first only to find his true voice. There was a silencing so that the sound of God could finally be heard once again. Eden's greatest pleasure, lost by Adam, was not the richness of the earth or the abundance of God's creation, but the voice of Him who would come walking in the cool of the day. The Father's voice that once spoke to Adam was found again that day by Job. He was rescued by the Father's love that day. That day Job became more like God because he was able to see God and His love. Job found his voice, and it was bold before God. Instead of Satan boldly confronting God, now Job spoke and God listened to him. I'll repeat Job's response here again:

> *Then Job answered the Lord, and said, I know that thou canst do every thing, and that no thought can be withholden from thee. Who is he that hideth counsel without knowledge? Therefore have I uttered that I understood not; things too wonderful for me, which I knew not.* ***Hear, I beseech thee, and I will speak: I will demand of thee, and declare thou unto me.*** *I have heard of thee by the hearing of the ear: but now mine eye seeth thee. Wherefore I abhor myself, and repent in dust and ashes.*
>
> —Job 42:1–6 KJV, emphasis mine

Job said to God, "I will demand of Thee." That sounds so brazen when you first read it. But in the passage, Job is repenting, and in the middle of his sorrow, a confidence we have not witnessed by Job before comes prodigiously exploding into this narrative. Job is now speaking to the living God and is boldly demanding from Him.

How did God respond to Job?

The Bible says that "the LORD accepted Job's prayer" when Job prayed for his friends, as we read earlier. Suddenly Job has God's ear. Job speaks to God as a king with inside knowledge. Satan was silenced when Job met God. Job stood that day without fear, unconcerned for himself. He stood as a priest-king and sacrificed the offerings that now meant something. These sacrifices were now the shadow of something Job had seen from afar; a soon-coming Messiah who would take away the sins of the world. Job saw Jesus in the whirlwind. Satan had a wind that destroyed Job and left him weeping and defeated on the dunghill of despair. God, ironically, answered in a whirlwind of His own. These were the mighty winds of redemption. These sacrifices were no longer offered by the inspiration of fear, but by the command of a God who loved Job, and Job knew it. Love cast out all fear. Job knew God's love. It was not just a feeling of love that Job experienced that day. He saw something. He saw God, and he saw Christ. He saw the Lamb slain before the foundation of the world. He saw how much God loved man and what He had planned from the very start. He saw what Jesus would do for him and his friends. It is interesting that Job does not only reference the things he heard God say from the whirlwind, but the fact that he saw God! He saw God, and he saw what his sacrifices of bulls and goats represented. They were shadows of the ultimate sacrifice. He suddenly had power in his sacrifices, like Abel, Noah, or Abraham. They meant something. They did something in heaven. They said something in the judgment hall of God. Job did not find himself free from Satan's scourge when he refused to curse God. He found no freedom even when he blessed the name of God amidst his insurmountable suffering. Ultimately, his liberation centered around his actions toward his friends. Freedom came, not in blessing God, but in blessing the people who had done him wrong. It was not enough to give God praise. There had to be a willingness to pray for those who had accused him. Eliphaz, Bildad, and Zophar had been unconscious extensions of Satan and his accusations, and Job had to pray for them and even sacrifice for them. In James 3:9 (KJV) we read:

> *Therewith bless we God, even the Father; and therewith curse we men, which are made after the similitude of God.*

To truly bless God, we must be able to bless men, who are the image and likeness of God. Job reversed the power of the devil when he blessed his fellow man, even people who had done him and God wrong. The devil lost his authority over Job when he acted in love toward his friend's bad behavior. If Job had blessed God but cursed his friends, it would have been like he had cursed God Himself. If bitterness had crept into his heart like a prowling rat looking for opportunity, it would have negated all the praise to God he could muster. Nevertheless, Job saw Jesus in the whirlwind, experienced the Father's love, and encountered the Spirit of the Living God. He emerged with power over the devil, power with God, and a prayer of mercy for his friends. The devil had lost. God revealed Himself to Job, and Job became a different man.

Today we are in a better place than Job. We have met Jesus and have been touched by the substance of His blood. We are seated in heavenly places in Christ. Satan is no longer our king, and we can find the same boldness and greater (than even Job) because Christ lives in us now. God is great, and now we can boldly say in Christ: "Greater is he that is in me than he that is in the world!" We are filled with the love of God that has been poured into our hearts by the great Holy Spirit. We are able to bless God, bless others, and bless ourselves with the blessing that God has given because of Jesus! May God bless you as you keep your eyes on Him!

Job:
A New Expanded Paraphrase and Intensified Translation

Job 1:1 Job (fatherless[2], hated), this is the name of a man who lived in the land called Uz. He was a righteous man, of complete integrity; respectfully devoted to God, avoiding every kind of evil.

---

2 Akkadian documents of the 2nd millennium b.c. from Mari, Alalakh, and Tell el-Amarna show a frequent use of this name. In the Execration Texts from Egypt (ca 2000 b.c.) a Palestinian chief has the name ʾybm. In a letter from Tell el-Amarna (no 256) a prince of Ashtaroth in Bashar is named Ay (y)âb. W. F. Albright (JAOS, 74 [1954], 223–233) suggests that the name means "where is (my) Father?" This etymology fits in well with Job's longing for God, who is hiding His face from His servant.[1]

Journal of the American Oriental Society

[1] Hartley, J.E. (1979–1988) "Job," *The International Standard Bible Encyclopedia*, Revised. Edited by G.W. Bromiley. Wm. B. Eerdmans.

1:2 He fathered seven sons and three daughters;

1:3 And his holdings included 7,000 sheep, 3,000 camels, 500 pair of oxen, 500 jennies (female donkeys), and he housed an abundance of servants. *This wealth* made him the most influential man among the sons of the East.

1:4 Now his sons hosted feasts, traveling to each man's house on his day (birthday, holy feast day) and they would send for their sisters, inviting them to eat and drink wine with them.

1:5 And so it happened, after the days of their festive drinking-parties were finished, Job sent and purified them. He would wake up early in the morning and offer up burnt sacrifices for each of them for Job said (*to himself*),"It is possible my sons have sinned and cursed (damned, renounced) God in their hearts. Thus Job did this constantly.

1:6 Now it was the Day (New Year's Day[3]) *when* the sons of God (sons of the Elohim, ruling spirits, gods[4]) entered (*heaven*), to take their places, in opposition[5] to the LORD;

---

3 6. *The day*. The Jerusalem Targum places this first heavenly assize on New Year's Day and the second (2:1) on the Day of Atonement. This is an entirely natural understanding in accordance with Jewish tradition. New Year's Day is the time of the preliminary judgment, when the good are immediately inscribed in the book of life and the wicked are blotted out. For those who are in-between, neither good nor bad, there is a period of grace until the Day of Atonement and then in a final judgment those fates previously undecided are fixed in accordance with each one's repentance.[1]

[1] Pope, M.H. (2008) *Job: Introduction, translation, and notes*. New Haven; London: Yale University Press (Anchor Yale Bible), p. 9.

4 *the gods*. Literally "sons of the gods." These are lesser members of the ancient pagan pantheon who are retained in later monotheistic theology as angels; cf. 38:7; Gen 6:2, 4; Pss 29:1, 89:7. In Ps 82:1 they are called simply "gods."[1]

[1] Pope, M.H. (2008) Job: Introduction, translation, and notes. New Haven; London: Yale University Press (Anchor Yale Bible), p. 9.

5 ע.ל־יהוה prep. (II 752; GK 119cc)-pr.n. (217) *before (against) Yahweh*[1]

[1] Owens, J.J. (1989) *Analytical key to the Old Testament*. Grand Rapids, MI: Baker Book House, p. 144.

accordingly Satan (the Accuser) entered with them (*as one of the sons of God*[6]).

1:7 And the LORD said to Satan (the Accuser): "Where have you come from?" And the Accuser answered the LORD:

---

6 Satan is part of the heavenly ruling court known as the "sons of God". These were not beings in the class of the Son of God or a born again son of God. These were angels that occupied places of authority in the Universe before God. Satan is called the "god of this world" in 2 Cor. 4:4. The Apostle Paul did not make up this title for Satan; rather there is a clarity to Satan's ruling position, found in the Old Testament scriptures and the language surrounding his activity. Paul was simply expounding upon what is clearly laid out in Job and other sacred writings in the Old Testament concerning Satan.

"From roving back and forth through the earth, walking about it (*in authority*[7])"

1:8 The LORD (*knowing all things*), said to Satan (the Accuser), "Yes or No? Have you *actually* set your heart (attention, focus) in opposition to my servant Job for there is none like him on the earth; a righteous man, of complete integrity; respectfully devoted to God, avoiding every kind of evil?"

1:9 Then Satan (the Accuser) answered the LORD saying, "Is it for nothing that Job fears God?"

---

[7] Satan said he was **roaming through** and walking **back and forth** on **the earth**, apparently looking for those whom he could accuse and dominate (1 Peter 5:8). Satan's **going** on the earth may also suggest his exercising dominion over it and its people. To walk on land often symbolized dominion over it (cf. Deut. 1:36; 11:24; Josh 1:3; 14:9). Satan, of course, is "the god of this Age" (2 Cor. 4:4; cf. Eph. 2:2) and "the whole world is under the control of the evil one" (1 John 5:19).[1]

[1] Zuck, R.B. (1985) "Job," in Walvoord, J.F. and Zuck, R.B. (eds.) *The Bible Knowledge Commentary: An Exposition of the Scriptures*. Wheaton, IL: Victor Books, p. 719.

Perhaps it is spoken proudly, and with an air of haughtiness, as if he were indeed the *prince of this world*, as if *the kingdoms of the world and the glory of them* were his (Lu. 4:6), and he had now been walking in circuit through his own territories.

Henry, M. (1994) *Matthew Henry's commentary on the whole Bible: complete and unabridged in one volume*. Peabody: Hendrickson, p. 656.

1:10 Have you, yourself, not fortified spiked barriers around him, and around all that pertains to his house, and around all that he possesses, whatever pertains to him in all directions? All of the work of his hands, you have blessed, and his wealth has erupted across the earth."

1:11 *Satan commanded*[8] *God saying*: "But extend your hand now! Strike everything that he owns! Then we will see whether he will bless or curse you to your face."

---

[8] The Satan suggests a test to prove his point.13 His language is abrupt; he commands God with imperative verbs: literally, 'But now, you just extend your hand and damage all his property.'[1]

[1] Andersen, F.I. (1976) *Job: An Introduction and Commentary*. Downers Grove, IL: InterVarsity Press (Tyndale Old Testament Commentaries), p. 89.

Then Satan challenges (commands) God to extend his hand against Job and destroy all Job's possessions.[1]

[1] Schultz, C. (1995) "Job," in *Evangelical Commentary on the Bible*. Grand Rapids, MI: Baker Book House (Baker reference library), p. 342.

1:12 Then the LORD said to Satan (The Accuser), "*According to your demand*[9], it is so; all that he has is in your power

---

[9] Many interpret this verse to represent God as setting boundaries to Satan's assault on Job. The entire context of Job chapters 1 and 2, when considered together, paint a different picture altogether. Demanding from God, Satan speaks to God as one in authority, within his rights to even command God to judge Job and the hedge around him. The Lord's language suggests that he is moved by Satan's imperatives to constrict the hedge in the exact way that Satan stipulates in the order. The negative prohibition stated by God is but contractual terminology similar to our modern "Not to Exceed" contracts. A "Not to Exceed" contract states certain parameters that are authorized in the contract. These parameters are established unambiguously by stating the limiting factor a party cannot exceed beyond. For example, a contractor may bill for services rendered up to a certain dollar amount. The contractual language will state this in some fashion, such as: "Contractor.A may bill for services rendered NOT TO EXCEED $50,000." In other words, "This is what we agreed to and not anything more than that which has been stated." The evidence for this, in the dialogue between God and Satan, is found in Job 2:3, when God states that "Satan moved him without cause," and Job 2:6, where the Lord appears to go back on His word (in Job 1:12) when Satan requires God to touch Job directly to attack him bodily. The moment Satan demands, once again, the Lord acquiesces to the very detail (namely hurting Job directly) that had been off-limits in the previous encounter in Job 1:12. This time God uses the same legal formula to indicate the terms of this engagement: "You may touch him but you will not kill him." This formulaic language captures, in condensed form, what God states as Satan moves God, once again, without cause. Satan never petitioned to kill Job. In fact, killing Job would have worked against Satan's ultimate purpose, to flush out Job's supposed desire to curse God when things did not go his way. If Job had cursed God, he would have died anyway. This is not God limiting Satan, but God as Judge, honoring the justified authority of Satan's claim; his claim being carried out to the letter of the law.

but you may not touch Job directly." So Satan (the Accuser) departed out of the presence of the LORD[10].

1:13 Then came The Day: Job's sons and his daughters were eating and drinking wine in the house of their eldest brother;

1:14 And a messenger came in to Job and said: "The cattle were plowing and the jennies (female donkeys) were grazing nearby,

1:15 when the Sabeans descended upon them and captured them. They struck down the servants with the edge of the sword and I alone escaped to report to you!".

---

10 Omniscience is very different from the Presence of God. Omniscience is an incommunicable attribute of God. It is true: that God is everywhere at all points of time and space equally. God can be fully 100 percent present in one locale and at the same time not diminish His capacity to be 100 percent present in another place in time and space or at all places at the same time. He is everywhere present, including in the universe and even in hell. The Presence of God described in Scripture is a special, revealed reality of God whereby someone can interact with, enter, and even leave that Presence. In the Old Testament, God's Presence is separated, holy, and primarily limited to isolated events or sanctified locations (i.e., Mount Sinai, Eden before the fall of man, the Temple, or heaven). Since this council is depicted in God's Presence, and there are no earth-based clues to its locale, it is assumed to be in heaven by most scholars. Also, Satan indicates to God that he had been on earth as opposed to where he was when he was speaking to God about his most recent excursions.

1:16 While the messenger was still speaking, another messenger came in and said, "The fire of Elohim (God) from heaven struck down, consuming the sheep and the servants in a violent blaze and I alone escaped to report to you!".

1:17 While the messenger was still speaking, another messenger came in and said, "The Kasdim (Chaldeans, horsemen) positioned themselves in three military companies and rushed down upon the camels, capturing them, and the servants, they struck down with the edge of the sword and I alone escaped to report to you!".

1:18 While the messenger was still speaking, another messenger came in and said, " Your sons and your daughters were eating and drinking wine in the house of their eldest brother;

1:19 when suddenly a great wind[11] came from across the desert and struck the four corners of the house and it fell upon the young people and they died and I alone escaped to report to you!".

1:20 And Job stood up, ripped his robe, shaved his head, collapsed to the ground, and worshipped;

---

[11] Heb. Lit.-a great spirit (possibly a tornado)

1:21 Saying, "Naked I came from my mother's womb, and naked I shall return. Yahweh gave and Yahweh has taken away; Blessed be the name of Yahweh.".

1:22 Throughout all of these *tragedies*, Job did not sin or commit blasphemy[12] against God.

2:1 Now it was the Day (the Day of Atonement[13]) *when* the sons of God (sons of the Elohim, ruling spirits, gods) entered (*heaven*), to take their places, in opposition to the LORD; accordingly Satan (the Accuser) entered with them (*as one of the sons of God*), to take his place, in opposition to the LORD.

2:2 And the LORD said to Satan (the Accuser): "Where have you come from?" And Satan (the Accuser) answered the LORD: "From roving back and forth through the earth, walking about it (*in authority*[14])"

---

12 The Arabic version is, *nor blasphemed God*; and the Targum, "neither did he set in order words of blasphemy before God;"

[1] Gill, J. (1810) *An Exposition of the Old Testament*. London: Mathews and Leigh (The Baptist Commentary Series), p. 200.

13 see Job 1:6 footnote

14 see Job 1:7 footnote

2:3 The LORD (*knowing all things*), said to Satan (the Accuser), "Yes or No? Do you (*still*) set your heart (attention, focus) in opposition to my servant Job; for there is none like him on the earth; a righteous man, of complete integrity; respectfully devoted to God, avoiding every kind of evil?" And he is still (immovable) holding tightly to his integrity even though you told (caused[15], commanded,

---

15 סות

swt, v., mislead, incite; incite against, entice away. 18×

Root: סות 1

Bible Senses

to incite (urge) *v., to urge on; cause to act*. Hifil: Jdg 1:14; 1 Sa 26:19; 1 Ki 21:25; Job 2:3; 2 Ch 18:2 (5×) *v*. verb

(2017) *The Lexham Analytical Lexicon of the Hebrew Bible*. Bellingham, WA: Lexham Press.

made, pushed[16], ordered[17]) me to consume him for no reason *or* purpose".

2:4 Then Satan (the Accuser) responded to the LORD saying, "Skin for skin, that is (to say)- all that the man owns will he surrender for his own life".

---

16 Although you moved me against him: the Hebrew verb rendered moved me is found in 36:18, "entice." It is used in 1 Kings 21:25, where Jezebel is said to "incite" her husband, King Ahab. Translations using "incite" are NEB, TOB, Pope, and Habel; NJB has "provoked," FRCL "pushed," and SPCL says "you made me…."

NEB New English Bible

TOB Traduction œcuménique de la Bible

NJB New Jerusalem Bible

FRCL French common language version

SPCL Spanish common language version

Reyburn, W.D. (1992) *A handbook on the book of Job*. New York: United Bible Societies (UBS Handbook Series), p. 57.

17 [3]And the Lord said to Satan, Thou hast therefore attended to my servant Job; that there is not of those on the earth a man like him, guiltless, true, unblameable, abstaining from all evil. Still he retaineth his innocence; so that thou hast ordered the destruction of his property, without accomplishing thy purpose.

Pells, S.F. (ed.) (1904) *The Old Covenant, Commonly Called the Old Testament: Translated from the Septuagint*. New Edition. Translated by C. Thomson. London: Skeffington & Son, p. Job 2:3.

2:5 *Satan commanded*[18] *God saying*: "Nevertheless, extend your hand now! Strike his bone and his flesh! Then we will see whether he will bless or curse you to your face."

2:6 Then the LORD said to Satan (The Accuser), "*According to your demand*[19], it is so; he is in your power. One thing only, you must preserve his life."

2:7 So Satan (the Accuser) departed out of the presence of the LORD[20] and struck Job with a tortuous inflaming disease (*probably deep boils or leprosy*) from the sole of his foot to the top of his head.

2:8 Then he (*Job*) grabbed a piece of a broken (*clay*) pot and scraped (*at the boils upon*) himself with it as he sat among the ashes[21].

---

18 see Job 1:11 footnote

19 see Job 1:12 footnote

20 see Job 1:12 footnote

21 LXX trans. "dung-hill"

2:9 [22]Then his wife said to him, "Are you still holding firm to your integrity?". *She demanded,* "Curse God and die!".

2:10 But he said to her, "Godless women talk in the same way as you are speaking! Also, we have received blessing from God; shall we not endure[23] the evil?". In everything, Job did not sin (*did not curse or blaspheme God*) with his lips.

---

22 LXX adds:

After a long time had passed his wife said to him: "How long will you endure and say, 'See, I will wait a bit longer, looking for the hope of my salvation.' Look, your memory is already blotted out from the earth [along with] the sons and daughters, the travail and pangs of my womb, whom I reared in toil for nothing. And you, you sit in wormy decay, passing the nights in the open, while I roam and drudge from place to place, and from house to house, waiting for the sun to go down, so that I may rest from my toils and the griefs which now grip me. Now, say some word against the Lord, and die." He, however, looked up and said to her, …

LXX The Septuagint

Pope, M.H. (2008) *Job: Introduction, translation, and notes*. New Haven; London: Yale University Press (Anchor Yale Bible), p. 22.

23 LXX trans.

2:11 Now when Job's three friends heard about all the calamity that came upon him, then each man came from his own home-region: Eliphaz the Temanite, Bildad the Shuhite, and Zopar the Naamathite- they had coordinated together to meet to mourn (sway back and forth) with him and to comfort him.

2:12 And when they lifted their eyes to look from a long way off and did not recognize him, they raised their voice and began to weep, each tore his robe (*in grief*), and (*mourning Job*) they threw dust on their heads and into the air.

2:13 Then they sat down with him on the ground, seven days and seven nights and no one spoke to him, not a word because they saw how intensely he anguished in pain.

About the Author

Matt and Tammy Donnelly are from Raleigh, North Carolina, where they founded Matthew Donnelly Ministries twenty years ago. They have served the Lord Jesus Christ faithfully as youth pastors, as associate pastors, as an itinerant evangelist, as mission workers, and now as an author. God has blessed them with three beautiful children who also serve in the ministry as children and teenagers. Their goal is to share liberating truths that connect people to God's love and life!

E-mail: mdmsurge@gmail.com

Look us up on Facebook and Instagram
@MatthewDonnellyMinistries

YouTube: